Wherever
There is a Problem,
There is
Money

Sunday Adelaja

Wherever There is a Problem, There is Money
©2017

ISBN 978-617-7394-14-2

London, United Kingdom
sundayadelajablog.com

This book is about the simple things that almost anybody can do. It is about the simple things that anyone can do to transform the problems around them to money, opportunities, jobs etc.

Wherever There is a Problem, There is Money
London, United Kingdom

Contents

Introduction

There are many books written on how to become rich and never have to worry about money again. The problem with many of them is that they tell you to do things that are often too hard for most people to do. And at times, they are not realistic for the average person on the street.

But this book is about the simple things that almost anybody can do. It is about the simple things that anyone can do to transform the problems around them to money, opportunities, jobs etc.

Finding your financial freedom is pretty easy, especially when you live in an environment with all sorts of problems. But most people would rather do things the hard way. Many will work hard all their lives living below their means, work hard for the rich and get entangled in the rat race and do what everyone else is doing rather than focus on coming up with solutions to problems.

The irony is that everyone is looking for money but they are running away from problems. How can you be looking for money and you are running away from problems? I mean, look at Africa and other developing countries around the world. Most people are running away from developing countries. Most people are running away from what they call poor countries. They are running away from countries they perceive to have too many problems.

But in the real sense, those countries where people are poor, where there are so many problems, there lies the richest goldmines.

And I can promise you that by the time you are done with the whole book; you will be aggressively looking for problems to solve. I am certain that you will be running back to the countries where people are running away from. I can assure you that you will become an employer and not an employee. And I can boldly tell you that while others are looking for jobs, you will be creating jobs.

Unfortunately, we are in a dispensation where problems have been defined incorrectly for us, and this calls for an urgent attention if we are to move forward. Problems are not bad. They are there for us. And I'm here to address the wrong mindset about problems. I'm here to address the notion that problems are bad. This book is here to tell you that the only reason why problems exist is for you and me. This book is here to tell you that where there is a problem, there is money.

Quite a good number of people are desperate for money. Everybody is looking for money, but they are looking for money through jobs alone. They have forgotten or they don't even know that the problems around them are goldmines that could yield a lot of money.

Problems are part of everyone's life. They sometimes seem to flood our lives without letting up, and we wonder if they will ever stop. None of us is immune to problems, or adversity. And the truth is, it's impossible to prevent.

However, we always have "opportunity" which arises from bad situations, if we are willing to learn from adversity and deal with it properly. With wisdom and a positive attitude, we can turn bad situations to our favor.

Because we cannot prevent bad situations from coming into life, it is imperative that we learn how to transform them into positive situations—turn life's lemons into lemonade. By employing the strategies of success at all times, we capitalize on the good and transform problems into something we can work with. Problems always have great opportunities hidden within them.

The world today is filled with a lot of people competing for jobs, rather than looking to see what problems are there to be solved. But I tell you this, if you will look to see what problem needs to be solved, and do what needs to be done to come up with a solution to the problem, then you will tap into God's abundance. Problems are opportunities that are waiting to be maximized. Solving problems is your sure way to a life of abundance.After reading this book, you will know that you have the ability to become very, very rich if you want to. Or at the barest minimum, you will find one or two things you can do that will make you richer if you so choose to do them.

So let's get started.

Sunday Adelaja
For The Love of God, Church, and Nation

CHAPTER 1

Problems Mean Different Things to Different People

Problems Mean Different Things to Different People

Have you ever wondered why the rich keep getting richer and the poor getting poorer especially during the times of crisis? Why is it that when there are a lot of problems and most people are suffering, some others are smiling to the bank? It seems as if you and I live in a world where problems seem to favor a few individuals and put most others down on their backs.

Take a look at this statistics from the Sunday Times Rich List and pay close attention to the period of time this wealth was acquired. According to the 2015 Sunday Times Rich List, Britain's billionaires have seen their net worth more than double since the recession, with the richest 1,000 families now controlling a total of £547 billion. Their assets have increased from £258 billion in 2009, a rise of more than 112%.

While average UK income earners have yet to recover from the worst economic crisis since the Great Depression, with thousands still flocking to food banks, the financial elite has emerged not only with their fortunes intact but holding a larger than ever slice of the cake.

The past 12 months saw the biggest bounce for the United Kingdom super-rich in six years, and London now has 80 billionaires, up from 72 last year – more than any other world city.

14

Oh! Doesn't it seem to go in the opposite direction of what you've always known or believe? Is recession not meant to affect everyone in the economy, both rich and the poor? Is that not the logical thing that should happen?

Then, why would a few individuals get richer when the economists and the entire specialists in the financial world said the economy is in a recession? Maybe the rich have a special machine that makes money for them in their rooms? But that would be illegal.

Let me show you more. In contrast to the soaring incomes of the richest, the Institute for Fiscal Studies think-tank says average household incomes have only recently recovered from the banking crash, leaving them no better off than in 2008. Median household income in the most recent financial year was at around the same level as it was in 2007–2008 before the recession, though still more than 2% below its 2009–2010 peaks.

The richest 1,000 families have more money than the poorest 40% of British households combined, according to the Equality Trust. Last year they saw their wealth increase by £28 billion, the equivalent of £77m a day.

You mean £77m a day? In a time of crisis? You mean some individuals could make so much even when there is no money in the economy? This got me thinking as well, so you are not alone.

"In bad times, the rich usually get richer."
–Stuart Wilde

But relax; this book has the answer – WHERE THERE IS PROBLEM, THERE IS MONEY. You've got the answer to this question in your hands right now. Therefore commit to reading to the very end, because by the time you are done reading, you will fall so much in love with problems.

By the time you read to the last page of this book, your mentality about problems will change forever. Your attitude about problems would have taken a 360 degree turn. Because I am about to reveal to you, what makes the rich get richer in times of crisis. You will begin to see every problem around you as a goldmine.

If some individuals could make a whooping £77m a day, there must be something they are doing right. If the time of recession is connected to increasing wealth and asset base of some individuals, there must be a correlation between problems and money. And if it comes during the time when there are a lot of problems, it should tell you something that there is a secret. That's the secret I'm about to reveal to you.

Just before that, I'll like to reveal more facts to you. I will also give you more statistics on how much some people make during times of crisis and in places where there are a lot of problems so that I can be sure we are on the same page and from there we can build on it.

Problems and Money Go Hand-In-Hand

It might also interest you to know that this £28 billion annual increase, approximately £77m a day is enough to foot the nation's council tax bills for a year, provide nearly 2 million living-wage jobs for a year or 1 million jobs paid at the average full-time wage of £27,195, said The Trust.

If some individuals could increase their wealth and asset base during times of recession, it proves that problems and money go hand in hand. It is a prove that money and problems have a cordial relationship. Those who understand this fact, increase their wealth and asset base during the crisis and those who don't understand this, go down with the economic recession.

«Problems are only opportunities in work clothes.»
—Henri Kaiser

Problems mean different things to different people. The rich see problems as opportunities to be grabbed. When they see problems, they see the money. They run to problems. And by solving these problems, they increase their wealth.

Since only a few individuals go out to solve the problems during the times of crisis, they will be the only ones to increase in wealth. That's why it seems that their money goes in the opposite direction to what the economy is saying. When the economy is down, they increase in wealth.

Take for example there is a scarcity of food in your country at the moment. Because of the scarcity, food prices will go up, which means everybody will spend more to be able to buy food stuff from the market, due to the increase in demand and low supply.

Now, imagine someone comes up with a way to solve this problem of scarcity of food. The person comes up with a way to mechanize production of food crops and makes food available to a larger group of people during this period. In essence, everybody goes to that personto buy food at a higher price. Now tell me, who will get rich during this time? Is it the people that complain about the scarcity of food or the person that solves the problem?

Definitely, the man who mechanizes food production will become rich. It is as simple as that. The same problem of food scarcity is experienced by everybody but within the same society, this problem was interpreted differently. While someone sought for the best way to solve this problem, the others did nothing.

Well, if it can be thought, it can be done, a problem can be overcome."
—E. A. Bucchianeri

The man who mechanized the food production actually overcame the problem and became richer through the same problem that made others cry and groan. This is the secret of getting richer in times of crisis and in places where there are a lot of problems. The succeeding pages and chapters of this book will also give you more practical examples as I unveil this secret to you.

The Rich Make Money Out of Problems

Let me also paint a similar picture for you in Africa. This is because while the media and everyone are painting Africa as a continent with so many problems, some individuals are still increasing in wealth in the same economy.

The Guardian's Africa wealth report 2015: *rich get richer even as poverty and inequality deepen* shows that the number of millionaires in Africa has more than doubled since the year 2000.

Africa is now home to more than 160,000 people with personal fortunes worth in excess of $1m (£642,000), a twofold increase in the number of wealthy individuals since the turn of the century that highlights the problem of deepening inequality as some of the world's poorest nations register strong economic growth.

The combined wealth holdings of high-net-worth individuals – those with net assets of $1m or more – in Africa totaled $660 billion at the end of 2014, according to a report by New World Wealth, a South African market research firm.

Meanwhile, the number of poor people in Africa – defined as those living on less than $1.25 a day – increased from 411.3 million in 2010 to 415.8 million in 2011, World Bank data shows.

By 2024, the number of African millionaires is expected to rise 45%, to approximately 234,000, according to the report.

During the past 14 years, the number of high-net-worth individuals in Africa has grown by 145%. The rate for the Middle East over the same period was 136%, while in Latin America it was 278%. The global average was 73%.

To the wise and people of understanding, they know that problem is their shortcut to wealth. The wise don't complain about problems, they make money out of problems. They turn people's problem to their enterprise. They've come to realize that where there is a problem there is money.

How do you respond to Problems?

Just in case you are yet to fully understand what I mean when I say problems mean different things to different people, let me show you here. The story of Bata Shoe Company will definitely do justice to this point and if you pay careful attention to every detail of the story, you will also discover the abundant wealth lying beneath problems.

Bata is one of the biggest shoe companies in Africa. At the end of the nineteenth century, just as colonial Africa was opening up as a market; all the manufacturers of shoes in Victorian England sent their representatives to Africa to see if there might be an opportunity there for their wares.

There was a shoe company before Bata that was sent to Africa to look into the African market of shoes. The representative that was sent to Africa then went to South Africa. He discovered that the Africans then were not putting on shoes.

This sales representative wrote back to his company telling them that there is no business in Africa. He reported that there is no business for them in Africa because Africans don't wear shoes. He considered it a waste of time and resources to try to do any kind of business in Africa.

The sales representative did not know the principle that if there is a problem there is business and money there. Whenever there is a problem, there is money. Problems give birth to money. Money is the by-product of problem.

The sales representative left the continent because he thought there was no business for his shoe company since Africans were not wearing shoes then.

Here is the point you need to read carefully. Bata Company sent their representative to survey Africa. This representative was a lot smarter. He gave a report that Africans don't wear shoes. But he added that it will be a big market for his company if they take responsibility for providing shoes for all Africans. He advocated for his company to send people to educate the African populace about the need to wear shoes.

Two different sales representatives were sent to Africa, but they saw the problem differently. The problem of not putting on a shoe meant different things to these two individuals, just like the biblical story of Caleb, Joshua, and the other ten spies, which I will discuss fully in the next chapter.

Now, you will see who made the money out of the problem. And this is exactly what goes on between the rich and the poor on a daily basis. That's why the rich get richer in times of crisis and anywhere there are problems.

I think you need to begin to question yourself right now on how you respond to problems. If you check your financial status, you might be able to pick a character that directly speaks to you from the stories I have shared with you so far. This will tell you which of the sales representative you are.

Problems mean different things to different people. How you respond to the problems around you will determine if the problem will work in your favor or against you. But it's a matter of choice. And the choice I am offering you today is to see a problem, seek for the solution and money will chase after you.

The lack of shoes gave birth to a company

"No problem can be solved from the same level of consciousness that created it."

-Albert Einstein

Bata Shoe Company fully understood what Albert Einstein meant here, therefore, they sent their educational team to sensitize Africans on the need to wear shoes.

The educational team of Bata Shoe Company came to Africa to educate the populace on the importance of putting on shoes; teaching them that it is better to put on shoes than to walk around barefooted.

Then, the company started a shoe factory in Africa and soon became the biggest shoe industry. They could now supply a whole continent with shoes. The lack of shoes gave birth to a company that the people now respect and hold in high esteem. The solution to the lack of shoes was their shortcut to wealth and prominence.

You might be thinking that people don't have money but wait until they have a problem. If you are really hungry, you will find money. If you truly seek knowledge, you will also get the money to be educated. Anywhere there is a problem, there is money.

If you have been long enough in Africa you must have come across the Safari boots. Originally designed in 1939, the desert boots from Bata, made of the finest cowhide and hand stitched at the Bata factory in Limuru, Kenya, where it was born, this original shoe remains unchallenged in its quality and popularity.

In Africa, you can find Bata stores in countries like Algeria, Angola, Botswana, Ethiopia, Ghana, Kenya, Lesotho, Malawi, Mauritius, Mozambique, Namibia, Republic of Congo, Rwanda, South Africa, Swaziland, Tanzania, Uganda, Zambia, Zimbabwe, Nigeria etc.

Bata dominates the African market. Their shops can be found even in the most remote part of Africa.

Bata operates in 5 continents.

Bata runs 27 production facilities across 20 countries.

Bata operates in over 70 countries.

Bata has over 5,000 stores worldwide.

Bata employs over 50,000 employees worldwide.

Bata serves over 1 million customers every day, worldwide.

Bata has over 20 in-house brands including the Safari boot which has remained a best seller throughout the decades.

There is a Bata nursery school in Limuru where children of Bata employees attend free of charge.

Bata came to Kenya in 1939 and set up a plant at Limuru. The Limuru factory has grown over the years and currently has the capacity to produce 60,000 pairs of shoes in a day.

Bata Kenya has 111 retail outlets.

Bata Kenya sells on average 30 million pairs of shoes in a year.

All these shouldn't be a surprise for a company that saw a problem; looked for a way to solve the problem and then the solution has produced a corporation. The story of Bata Company attests to the fact that wherever there is a problem, there is money.

Where there is problem, there is abundance of wealth

There was a problem in Africa, the other companies who we don't know of today ran away from such problems. Bata, on the other hand, seized the opportunity, solved the problem by educating the populace on the need to wear shoes and provided the shoes. Isn't that easy enough for anyone to do? How difficult is that?

This is the same attitude that makes the rich get richer. Every truly successful individual or business is solving a problem. No problem solver can end up in poverty. Where there is a problem, there is an abundance of wealth.

Those that see problems as opportunities, run towards the problem to solve it and create a business out of that solution will always get richer. While those who see problems as a bad omen, run away from problems and never think of a way to solve problems will always get poorer. It is a fact of life.

Therefore, those who look for solutions in times of crisis will always get richer no matter what the economy says. And that is exactly what those that are rich do. The economy doesn't dictate the money in your pocket, the problems you solve does. The rich get richer by solving the problems around them. The poor get poorer by doing nothing about the problems around them.

"Do not focus on money; instead focus on a problem that needs to be solved for the world...money will follow you as a by-product."
-Manoj Arora

Money is always connected to problems. Money is a by-product of problems. There is a cordial relationship between problems and money. Money and problems are relatives.

The child of problem is solution and the grandchild of problem is money. Problems must give birth to solutions, then, the solution leads to money. Problem, therefore, is a wealthy goldmine. And where there is a problem, there is money.

Problem → Solution → Money

I will continue to elaborate on this in the next chapter especially the different definitions people give to problems. In this chapter, you've seen the difference between the rich and the poor and you now understand why the rich get richer and the poor get poorer in times of crisis. But I am about to build on that and I will show you the consequences of seeing problems from the other side of the coin.

The two sides of the coin are what you've just read about and I believe the story of Bata Shoe Company did justice to that. They became richer because they solved a problem. Unfortunately, the company which we don't even know of ran away and did nothing about the same problem that Bata Shoe Company took responsibility for and solved it.

"Problems are meant to be solved, but unfortunately, a lot of people choose to complain, worry, and cry about them."
-Edmond Mbiaka

In the next chapter, I will give you more practical examples and you will see the consequences of doing nothing about problems. It's not enough to get poorer if you do nothing about the problems around you, there are more devastating consequences.

Nuggets

1. You might be thinking that people don't have money but wait until they have a problem.

2. Every truly successful individual or business is solving a problem.

3. Those that see problems as opportunities, run towards the problem to solve it and create a business out of that solution will always get richer.

4. The economy doesn't dictate the money in your pocket, the problems you solve does.

5. Money is always connected to problems. Money is a by-product of problems.

6. There is a cordial relationship between problems and money. Money and problems are relatives.

7. Problems must give birth to solution, then, solution leads to money.

Problem → Solution → Money

CHAPTER 2

Confronting the wrong mindset about problems

Confronting the wrong mindset about problems

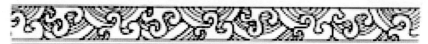

The problem of not putting on a shoe meant different things to two different individuals in the last chapter. They saw the same problem but gave it different meanings. Their outlook and mindset on the same problem produced different results because they see the problem differently. Therefore, we can come to a conclusion that…

"The way we see the problem is the problem."
-Stephen R. Covey

In the same light, I will share a very interesting lesson with you in this chapter in the hope that you will begin to see problems from the right lens and from the right perspective.

Problems have been defined incorrectly for us, and this calls for an urgent attention if we are to move forward. Problems are not bad. They are there for us. They are opportunities that are waiting to be maximized. Solving problems is your sure way to a life of abundance.

The rich understood this, that's why they are getting richer and the poor have failed to learn or those who know have failed to practice what they know, that's why they are still poor. The rich move very fast to solve problems when it arises but the poor are most often inactive waiting for a miracle to turn the tables in their favor.

But I'm here to address a wrong mindset about problems. I'm here to address the notion that problems are bad. This book is here to tell you that the only reason why problems exist is for you and me. This book is here to tell you that where there is a problem, there is money.

Money answers to problems. Money follows problems. Money will chase you if you can come up with solutions to problems. Although, that is not my main concern in this chapter. That is not the subject of discussion in this chapter because I will like to correct the wrong mindset you have about problems before we can build on it.

There are also grievous consequences when you remain inactive towards a problem you are meant to solve. And that is what this chapter is here to address. So, stay tuned!

Lessons Learned From the Twelve Spies

After the children of Israel were freed from the Egyptian bondage and delivered from Pharaoh's army, they began their journey toward Mount Sinai. In the wilderness, God provided food, water, and protection.

It was recorded in the Bible that they have just been rescued out of 400 years of slavery. They had walked through the Red Sea and had watched the Egyptian army drown. They had been miraculously guided through the wilderness, and been promised a land flowing with milk and honey.

Miracle after miracle. Blessings after blessings. All they had to do was just to trust and obey God. In summary, they had all their problems solved for them miraculously.

When they arrived at Sinai, they received the law that would govern them as a nation and the pattern for the tabernacle regulating their worship. After being numbered and organized, they were now ready to enter the land of promise.

And then, God wanted to see how they would respond to a problem when they encounter one. Because I tell you this very seriously if you have the wrong mindset about problems, it is difficult to see solutions, and if you can't see the solution to a problem, then, you are not ready for a positive change. It shows that you are not ready for growth and your status will remain the same if not worse.

However, it seems that the people originated the idea to search the land. Eleven days after God gave them His Law and His promises, the children of Israel arrived at the border of the Promised Land. Moses and Aaron chose 12 men - the top leaders out of hundreds of thousands - to explore the land and see if God was telling the truth.

God agreed to it and told them to «*spy out the land*» and see how the people lived, how strong they were, and what the land looked like. After forty days, the spies returned and admitted Canaan was a wonderful land but expressed doubt they could conquer these strong people.

Two of the spies, Caleb and Joshua, objected and said, «we are well able» to take the land. However, the majority prevailed and Israel wandered in the wilderness another 38 years while an entire generation died.

What a devastating blow! What a tragedy! An entire generation of the army that crossed the Red Sea and had watched the Egyptian army drown. An entire generation that went through the wilderness only to get the border of the Promised Land and lose everything they had worked for to a wrong attitude they had towards problems.

"While we are free to choose our actions, we are not free to choose the consequences of our actions."
-Stephen R. Covey

The last chapter showed you an example of what solving a problem can do. Right now, I'm presenting to you what devastating consequences a wrong attitude to problems can also cause.

So what example is set for us in this account? What admonitions do we receive? What lessons do we learn from the twelve spies?

Two Attitudes

The outlook of the ten spies was not very bright. They had the wrong attitude towards the problem. They were like the other sales representative sent to survey Africa for their Shoe Companies and they came back that there was no market for their company in Africa because Africans don't wear shoes.

The report the ten spies gave was one of gloom. They could only see the problems instead of the possibilities, the giants instead of God and defeat instead of victory. The inspired writer called it «an evil report.»

"And they brought up an evil report of the land which they had searched unto the children of Israel, saying, The land, through which we have gone to search it, is a land that eateth up the inhabitants thereof; and all the people that we saw in it are men of a great stature."
Numbers 13:32 (KJV)

Their attitude could certainly be called negative. And this is the attitude we've been fed with and this chapter is out to address it. This is the attitude most poor individuals have towards problems. They never ever see a solution to a problem. They never see the light at the end of the tunnel.

On the other hand, Caleb and Joshua were very optimistic individuals. Caleb and Joshua are analogous to the Bata Shoe Company sales representative. Their report was one of hope. They saw the possibilities instead of the problems, God instead of giants, and victory instead of defeat. God said Caleb «had a differentspirit.» Yes, it was different from the ten spies because it was positive instead of negative.

There's a heavy-duty lesson for us how the 12 spies reacted to the Promised Land. Remember, these 12 men traveled throughout the same land. They saw the same things. But they came to two very different conclusions.

The sales representatives sent to survey Africa saw and knew that Africans don't wear shoes, but only one recognized the possibility buried in that problem. Similarly, Joshua and Caleb saw scary things and trusted God, encouraging the Israelites to believe God's promises:
> **«Let us go up at once and take possession, for we are well able to overcome»**
>
> (Num. 14:30).

The other 10 spies saw scary things and doubted God (v. 31-33):
> **«We are not able to go up against the people, for they are stronger than we.»**

They said they saw giants «and we were like grasshoppers in our own sight ...» A replica of the other sales representatives that did not see any opportunity for their companies in Africa.

Today, in the world and in the church, we still have these two groups of people. Some, which are very few, can see opportunities, possibilities, solutions to problems and the disposition that says «we are able.» While there are others who seem to be the majority today, who can only see their inability, the flaw in any idea and say «we are not able.» And that is the reason why this negative attitude needs to be addressed.

Traits of the Ten Spies

Let us take a closer look into this negative attitude of the ten spies and see what traits composed their character.

• Doubt. They said, «*We are not able.*» Doubt caused them to question their resources to take the land, as well as their God who was leading them.

What if Bill Gates, Microsoft co-founder had doubted his vision of living in a world where people own personal computers? Or the Wright brothers who built and flew the first aircraft believed they were not able? What kind of world are we going to live in today?

• Self-depreciation.
«*We are in our own sight as grasshoppers, and so we were in their sight*»

(Num. 13:33).

They saw themselves as teeny, tiny, little grasshoppers about to be squashed by the big, bad giants. Just as a lot of people today see themselves as incapable or incompetent of being a solution to the problems ravaging their society. They see the problem as a giant about to crush them.

• Fear. Joshua indicated in Numbers 14:9 that they were afraid. Fear naturally follows doubt and self-depreciation. Fear then will paralyze one and keep him from acting.

• Critical spirit. When people become negative and inactive, they turn to criticizing others who want to move forward. The whole congregation was influenced by these terrible ten to murmur and complain against God's leaders, Moses and Aaron.

• Unbelief. All of these negative traits can be summed up in one word - unbelief.

My dear brother and sister, doesn't it scare you to death to look at this list and see so many of these negatives in the society and in the church today, attitudes that hold us back, that divide our ranks, that cause us to wander in the wilderness of poverty and keep us from entering the land of promise? Doesn't it scare you to look at the list above and see that we are the ones holding ourselves back?

We've got to wake up and address this negative attitude to problems in our societies, churches, mosques and schools. It is an urgent call and we have to do something about it.

I'm not out to bash the church but I must say it as it is. The church has been a breeding place for this attitude and it must stop. The people must be educated that problems are opportunities waiting to be grabbed. The people must be told that one of the surest ways to their financial fortune is solving problems. The people must be sensitized on how to think critically and analytically to solve their own problems instead of running away from it or leaving everything to God.

Addressing the Negative Attitude to Problems

Although little discussed, one of Europe's greatest achievements was the successful imposition of Christianity on the people it conquered, enslaved and colonized in Africa.

It is difficult to point out where things went awry, but along the road, Christianity in Africa lost its innocence. The traditional Christian sects – Roman Catholicism, Anglican, and Methodist were pushed aside by a more ferocious form of fundamental Pentecostal Christianity.

Unlike the Old-School church leaders who were contended to keep a low profile, the new Priests were as aggressive as they are garrulous. Unlike in the Old churches where the Protestants were more concerned about an increase in entrepreneurship that solves problems for the people, helped to build schools and clinics, today's religious sects have no interests in such mundane stuff.

The Old church believed in a total detachment from superstitions, civilization, and industrialization. They know that money and wealth is a by-product of diligence, hard work, sacrifice, faith, and passion.

But before long Pentecostal churches sprang up all over cities, town, and villages preaching the Gospel of Crass Materialism. The new priests have absolutely no compunction in breaking laws in proclaiming their Gospel of Prosperity. Whereas the Old Priests frown on materialism, the New Pastors believe in loudly proclaiming their new-found affluence.

And with this wealth came acceptance, so much so that the very rich ones among the pastors became laws unto themselves. They put up church buildings wherever they wish. They break laws, rules, and regulations at will. They can stop traffic to hold jamborees. They care little for laws and hold all-night vigils in residential areas, where they keep citizens awake all night with their loud music. Whereas that time could have been invested in coming up with solutions to the problems eating the society up.

Because they hold sway over thousands of Congregants, many of the Pastors become very powerful people in society and become friends with political leaders. Presidents and Ministers courted them assiduously.

It is difficult to know whether it was religion that corrupted politics in Africa or the other way around, what is not debatable today is that Christianity has indeed become

become an Albatross that is strangling the life out of Africa.

Religion has turned many Africans into unthinking Zombies who, with childlike helplessness, wait for the intervention of God for the supply of basics like water, food, and electricity. Citizens have been persuaded not to hold elected officials responsible for their inactions to provide basic services. Because of religion, leaders no longer feel any need to fulfill election promises made to citizens. All they need to do is to turn citizens' eyes into the sky, to await the interventions of 'God,' while they do nothing.

"Many people find it socially and morally advantageous to hypocritically profess their religious beliefs, and to use religion to justify what they want to believe and do."

– Dr T.P.Chia

Take a close look at these examples:

Praying for Ebola: A few years ago, the dreaded EBOLA disease ravaged the West African countries of Guinea, Liberia and Sierra Leone. The last two countries were just emerging and recovering from devastating wars.

With much of the health infrastructures destroyed by the conflict, they clearly lacked the capacity to cope with a fast-spreading epidemic. That was understandable.

What was difficult for citizens of Liberia to fathom was the declaration by their president, Madam Helen Sirleaf Johnson, of seven days of fasting and prayers.

Many asked what exactly Madam President expected to happen after the fasting and praying pyrotechnics. Luckily, the international community mobilized to help the affected countries.

Praying for Zambian Kwacha: Liberia was not the only African country where leaders seek divine intervention in the affairs of man. The meltdown in the global economy resulted in the collapse in demand for Zambian main export, Copper. With the capacity to earn foreign exchange greatly reduced, the value of local currency, the Kwacha, collapsed.

And instead of seeking solutions, the president in a bid to appease the lamentations of citizens, called for three days of prayers to help shore up the value of the sinking currency. Many Zambians were not amused.

> *"Among politicians the esteem of religion is profitable; the principles of it are troublesome."*
> – Benjamin Whichcote

Praying for Fuel Scarcity: Nigeria is Africa's largest producer of crude oil. The country derives more than half of its income from the export of crude oil. Yet, for some unfathomable reasons, Nigeria periodically suffers from fuel scarcity.

So acute was the latest bout of scarcity that a leading Pastor called on Nigerians to close shop and hold special prayer to help with the fuel scarcity. The pastor refused to say whether he expects crude to raindown from the sky or for angels to repair the country's three refineries.

Our Nations Need 'Calebs' and 'Joshuas'

With this attitude of praying for everything and using our brains to do nothing or tapping the intellectual potentials in the country, how are we going to ever belief in the potentials God placed in us? Somebody, please tell me, why won't doubt thrive? Why are we not going to live in the fear of what tomorrow holds? In a society like this, why won't the traits of the ten spies be the order of the day? I need an answer, please!

If we go to God for everything even for clean water and basic amenities, when are we going to ever exercise our minds to think solutions? When are we going to be able to come up with African solutions to African problems?

> *"Many people pray to be kept out of unexpected problems.*
> *Some people pray to be able to confront and overcome them."*
> -Toba Beta

While we are been fed with the message of praying for everything, even the problems we can solve ourselves, nations who don't even believe in God are offering us aids. Isn't this an irony? Isn't it laughable that we earnestly pray to God, yet we lack basic amenities for life?

Will I now be wrong to say that while we are busy praying to be kept out of problems, other nations that are offering us aids and setting up gigantic companies in our continent are praying for the ability to confront and overcome these problems? Will I be wrong to say that while we lock ourselves up in night vigils, other nations around the world are solving our problems for us and thereby getting richer?

Dear reader, we need to begin to believe in ourselves and look inside, because we have the solutions. These myriads of problems are shortcuts to wealth for the continent. The solution to these problems will bring us money than we can fathom. This wrong attitude to problems must be addressed. It must be confronted. We need 'Calebs and Joshuas.'

I am not demeaning prayers. God answers prayers. I am a testimony to the fact that God answers prayers both for me as an individual and the congregation God has blessed me with.

But before you stone me, have you thought of the fact that the same God that drowned Pharaoh and his army and fell the wall of Jericho did nothing when it was time to take over the Promised Land? Did it come to your mind that the same God that spoon fed the Israelites in the wilderness with daily manna wanted them to conquer the Promised Land themselves?

This negative attitude to problems is an elephant on the road to progress; a millstone around the neck of usefulness; a cancer of the mind of its advocate; and an ice pack on the fervor of the faithful. It sees thorns on the rose bush, never the roses on the thorn bush. Its parent is little faith, its child is discouragement, its grandchild is cantankerousness and its first cousin is stubbornness!

And I beg to ask, did the fuel scarcity in Nigeria or the economy improve because of the prayers offered? What about the Zambian Kwacha? Yes, it's good to pray but this same 'good thing' can be bad when we leave everything to prayer and do nothing about the problem on ground.

«*The problem is not that there are problems. The problem is expecting otherwise and thinking that having problems is a problem.*»
— Theodore Rubin

This negative attitude has kept Africa in abject poverty while we are surrounded by problems that are urgently crying for solutions. If only we can wake up now and begin to use our minds more than ever before. If only we can see how much other nations are making by solving their own problems. The problems on our continent are the numerous blessings of God to provide us with abundant wealth that eyes have not seen and ears have not heard.

Caleb and Joshua

This chapter wouldn't be complete if I fail to tell you about Joshua and Caleb. These two men were «different.» They had a different disposition, a different focus on life, and a different attitude towards the problem facing their nation. What were some of the attributes of their attitudes?

• Faith. They said,
«We are well able to overcome»
(Num. 13:30).

They believed in themselves, and in their fellow Israelites. They knew God was with them but more importantly, they also know that the problem of conquering the Promised Land was their responsibility.

• Confidence. Concerning the Canaanites, Joshua said,

«The people are bread for us: their defense is departed from them, and the Lord is with us»
(Num. 14:9).

They had the confidence in the outcome of this undertaking because they knew they were doing the will of God. It is the will of God that we become problem solvers in our nation and everywhere we find ourselves.

• Courage. Joshua said,
«Fear them not»
(Num. 14:9).

He was not afraid of the giants, the walled cities or the strength of the people.

• Action. Caleb said,

«Let us go up at once, and possess it»

(13:30).

Problem solvers say,

«Let's go and do it now!»

• Appreciation. They understood the land was a gift from God, a blessing due to his delight in them. True appreciation for one's blessings will lead to action and obedience. They knew the Promised Land was a gift and a blessing from God. They understood that though it posed a problem to them at first if the problem could be solved they will be launched into a world of abundance, a land that flowed with milk and honey.

"Every problem is a gift - without problems, we would not grow."

-Anthony Robbins

Today, as we face the giant problems around us, this is the attitude that should govern our lives. We need the positive traits of faith in our abilities, confidence, and courage, coupled with action and an appreciation of God's blessings to lead us on to victory. We need 'Calebs' and 'Joshuas.'

Don't be a whiner! Be a winner for God!

It was recorded that there were 603,550 men of war. Of that number only two, Caleb and Joshua, entered into Canaan. That means 603,548 fell in the wilderness. That is the grievous consequence of having a negative attitude to problems. The problem you refuse to solve might come back hunting you. Beware!

Will you decide today to develop the disposition like God's two heroes of old? Or will you be like those shameful spies who brought back the negative report? Don't be a whiner! Be a winner for God!

Indisputably, there is the role of God in the affairs of men but yet there is the role of man in the affairs of this world as well. Come to think of it what if Thomas Edison, the man who made it possible for electric light bulbs to last long hours or Alexander Bell, the telephone inventor or Bill Gates who made it possible for everyone to own a personal computer decided not to confront the problems they solved for the world? Are we going to be talking about Bill Gates as the richest man in the world today?

What if Aliko Dangote, an entrepreneur and presently the richest African or Mike Adenuga, the CEO of Globacom telecommunications in West Africa decided to adopt the praying mentality of the average African, and wait for God's intervention, what would have happened to their wealth? What if they adopted the negative attitude to the problems in Nigeria like the ten spies or the other sales representatives?

Imagine our world today without electric bulbs? From the electric bulb in your room to the incandescent lamps in your office or your car head lamp, are we still going to the living in a world of darkness?

Bill Gates is the richest man in the world today, imagine if he had said to himself many years ago, that the problem of personal computers is a giant and he sees himself as a grasshopper, how would you be reading this book today?

Be the Joshua and Caleb of your generation

"I truly believe in positive synergy, that your positive mindset gives you a more hopeful outlook, and belief that you can do something great means you will do something great."

My dear brothers and sisters, there is a wrong attitude to problems that need to be addressed. Don't be like the ten spies. Don't have the disposition of the sales representatives sent to survey Africa. This is the wrong mindset you and I have to confront and defeat it.

Be the Joshua and Caleb of your generation. Have a positive outlook. This positive synergy has a way of being infectious to everyone in your environment. See the opportunities, the possibilities, and the solutions.

"Once your mindset changes, everything on the outside will change along with it."

\- Steve Maraboli

Bill Gates solved a problem, the result is glaring. Steve Jobs, the founder of Apple Computers Company solved a problem of making computers portable and easy to use for the average man, he died a billionaire. Mike Adenuga, the second richest man in Nigeria is a billionaire in US dollars, thanks to the problem he solved by providing access to telecommunications to millions in West Africa.

My message to you today is that where there is a problem, there is money. Where there is a problem, there is a job waiting for you. Where there is a problem, there are enormous opportunities and possibilities. You are the determining factor. Go ahead and do great things.

In the succeeding chapters, I will be showing you how to identify a solution that you have been specifically built to tackle and subdue. You are surrounded with myriads of problems and that signifies wealth all around you. Where there is a problem, there is money.

If the rich choose to be solving more problems, they will continue to get richer. And if the poor choose to be inactive and wait for some miracle, they will continue to get poorer. Problems are blessings in disguise. They are there for you.

Nuggets

1. We can come to a conclusion that…*the way we see the problem is the problem.*

2. Problems are not bad. They are there for us. They are opportunities that are waiting to be maximized.

3. Solving problems is your sure way to a life of abundance.

4. The rich move very fast to solve problems when it arises but the poor are most often inactive waiting for a miracle to turn the tables in their favor.

5. Money answers to problems. Money follows problems. Money will chase you if you can come up with solutions to problems.

6. If you have the wrong mindset about problems, it is difficult to see solutions, and if you can't see the solution to a problem, then, you are not ready for a positive change.

7. Religion has turned many Africans into unthinking Zombies who, with childlike helplessness, wait for the intervention of God for the supply of basics like water, food, and electricity.

8. The problem you refuse to solve might come back hunting you. Beware!

CHAPTER 3

Take Advantage of the existing Problems

Take Advantage of the existing Problems

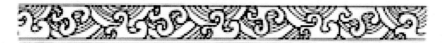

Having understood the different meanings people give to problems and the consequences of seeing a problem from the other side of the coin, it's time to build on it.

Let's take it a bit further as we look at how other developed and some developing countries are taking advantage of the problems in Africa. They are investing heavily in the continent and making a lot of money, while the continent is living in abject poverty. The irony of everything is the fact that while Africans are complaining there is no money in the continent, foreign companies who recognize the relationship between problems and money are making millions of dollars.

Maybe this will paint a better picture for you. Take a look at the number of Chinese firms in the following African countries according to the AFKInsider.

Nigeria
Number of projects: 404
Number of firms: 240

South Africa
Number of projects: 280
Number of firms: 152

Zambia
Number of projects: 273
Number of firms: 125

Ethiopia
Number of projects: 255
Number of firms: 114

Egypt
Number of projects: 197
Number of firms: 99

This is just about Chinese firms alone operating on the continent. We've not mentioned the likes of American, Japanese, or German firms.

I don't want the statement 'Taking advantage of the problems in Africa' to be misleading here. But is that not the truth? Are they doing anything wrong? Because while we are waiting for supernatural interventions to give us good roads, put food on our tables and provide good and affordable houses for the populace, they are developing machinery that can solve these problems effectively.

«Each problem has hidden in it an opportunity so powerful that it literally dwarfs the problem. The greatest success stories were created by people who recognized a problem and turned it into an opportunity.»
-Joseph Sugarman

There is Money in Africa

It is no longer news that Africans have accepted their fate and learnt to live with epileptic power supply, bad roads, terrible health facilities and poor infrastructures. In fact, Epileptic public power supply and household quest to obtain power from alternative sources have become a daily occurrence in Nigeria, Africa's most populous country.

Some interesting statistics on the usage of power generating sets in Nigeria has been revealed in 2014 by the Director-General of Centre for Management Development, Dr. Kabir Usman. According to him, about 60 million Nigerians spend N1.6 trillion (running into millions of US dollars on the average) on generators annually.

He also said that Nigeria had the highest number of standby generators, which had become permanent, making the Power Holding Company of Nigeria (PHCN) the standby.

It might interest you to know that all these generating sets being talked about here are not manufactured in the country, not even in the continent. We have left this problem for the foreign companies to solve. They have discovered an opportunity in the midst of this problem.

«In the middle of difficulty lies opportunity.»
-Albert Einstein

Now tell me, who get the millions of US dollars annually? Is it the countries that manufacture the generating sets and export it to Africa? Or Africans who are locked up in churches around the continent waiting for God to fix the power sector and only complain that the politicians are corrupt?

"*Currently, there are about 60 million generators in Nigeria at the ratio of one per household of 2.5 people,*" the Nigerian Tribune Newspaper quoted him as saying at the launch of the National Power Training Institute of Nigeria (NAPTIN) graduate skills developmentprogram in Abuja. It is further noted that the presence of too many generators has also been the cause of many deaths in the nation as a result of carbon monoxide emission.

Still, on the use of generating sets as alternative sources of electricity, it is no news that irregular power supply has adversely affected businesses in Nigeria. He revealed that Nigeria's highly inadequate supply of electricity adds 40 percent to the cost of goods produced in the country. According to him, "*the situation has compelled many industries to either shut down or relocate to neighboring countries.*"

I know it is a very popular belief that the continent is poor, but with these facts and figures, I beg to disagree. There is money in the continent; we are not solving the problems ourselves. When we allow others solve these problems for us, they only become richer at our expense.

Problems equates money

I got to fully realize this relationship between problems and money about 20 years ago when things in Ukraine were so bad. The economy was so bad. Everything was a mess after the collapse of communism. Communism came down. The country was a great mess and everything was falling apart. The average salary a month was $10. Things were so bad. People were living in abject poverty.

During this period in the country, I had some businessmen visit me from Germany. While we were discussing, they told me that we have so much money in this country. I was perplexed. What! The people are suffering. People are hungry.

But they opened my eyes to see the problems in the country, making me understand that the solution to these problems facing the country was a goldmine waiting to be dug. They said, "There is no road and that is an opportunity to make money." The roads were bad, that is money. They saw problems and they knew that problems equate to money.

«Opportunities! They are all around us. There is power lying latent everywhere waiting for the observant eye to discover it.»
-Orison Swett Marden

Also, during that period in the country, garbage and dirt were everywhere on the street. They saw a business opportunity in this also. Somebody could come up and bring a solution to the problem of clearing the garbage. If someone else comes and fix the roads, that is a lot of money. There were no street lights also; someone could come up with an idea or develop a more efficient technology to fix this.

And this is exactly what the foreign companies in Africa are doing. They are taking advantage of the problems in the continent. That is what Bata Shoe Company did many years ago and today they are giants in the Shoe making industry in the continent. Their companies are thriving because of the enormous demands for their products in the continent.

"What I taught myself was that in any problem you get, you've got to come up with an innovative, brilliant, kind of unusual, stunning solution."
-George Lois

Using China as a good example here, Chinese products have flooded markets in Johannesburg, Luanda, Lagos, Cairo, Dakar and other cities, towns, and villages in Africa. This is because they are very innovative and they put their brilliant minds to work to come up with solutions to the pressing problems and demands in Africa. Those goods include clothing, jewelry, electronics, building materials and much more. Even little things like matches, tea bags, children's toys and bathing soaps are coming from China. In fact, you can still see *'made in China'* on some of the plates we use in eating around the continent.

Chinese industries require new markets for their products and Africa is a potentially enormous outlet. China has been so far successful in coming up with ways to provide solutions to the problems in Africa. China is repositioning itself continuously for the new Africa that's emerging.

They are also pushing other competitors away aggressively because African consumers like Chinese products due to the fact that they are affordable. Chinese goods are cheaper than those from Europe and North America.

Africa became an easy, convenient target, topping the Beijing economic agenda. Year after year, Chinese leaders headed business delegations to every major African capital, landing infrastructure projects and trade deals, which turned Africa into China's "second continent."

With trade between China and its second continent reaching close to $200 billion in 2013, which doubles the trade level between the United States and Africa. And in 2011, trade between Africa and China was $166 billion, according to the *Economist*, a UK weekly.

China's gift to Africa

However, it is disheartening in the twenty first century that the new headquarters of the African Union (AU), a towering 20-storey building in Addis Ababa, Ethiopia, is so called "China's gift to Africa" because China picked up the

$200 million tab for the state-of-the-art complex. Ethiopia's tallest building, completed in December 2011 in time for an AU summit the following month, includes a 2,500-seat conference hall.

This is an insult and a disgrace to the African Union and to every African that in 2012 a building as symbolic as the AU headquarters is designed, built and maintained by a foreign company.

China had either donated or assisted in building a hospital in Luanda, Angola; a road from Lusaka, Zambia's capital, to Chirundu in the southeast; stadiums in Sierra Leone and Benin; a sugar mill and a sugarcane farm in Mali; and a water supply project in Mauritania, among other projects.

It is heart breaking to see that a contract to build a stadium in Lusaka, Zambia's capital is awarded to a Chinese company. It is a pity that a sugar mill and a sugarcane farm in Mali have to be built by the Chinese firms. This is how much foreign companies are taking advantage of the problems in the continent to get richer. Since most of our resources are spent on foreign companies which will be definitely more expensive than local companies, why won't these countries get richer and the African continent get poorer?

In an article in This Is Africa, a Financial Times publication, it was stated that in recent years China's economy at times has grown at more than 10 per cent a year, while cheap labor has helped reduce production costs, hence cheaper products. They also noted that the low level of the Yuan [the Chinese currency] compared to the other major world trading currencies such as the US dollar, the euro and the yen attracts African importers.

Already trade between Africa and China has grown at a breathtaking pace. It was $10.5 billion in 2000, $40 billion in 2005 and $166 billion in 2011. China is currently Africa's largest trading partner, having surpassed the US in 2009.

Also, Chinese construction firms are acquiring enormous construction contracts. The China Railway Construction Corporation (CRC) signed a $1.5 billion contract in September 2012 to modernize a railway system in western Nigeria. That same month, China South Locomotive and Rolling Stock Corporation, thelargest train manufacturer in China, signed a $400 million deal to supply locomotives to a South African firm, Transnet. In February 2012 the CRC announced projects in Nigeria, Djibouti, and Ethiopia worth about $1.5 billion in total.

Oh! How I wish Africans understood this! How I wish we knew that where there is a problem, there is money. So far as long as we stay idle and do nothing or wait for God to come and do something about the problems in the country, nothing will happen.

I don't need to be a prophet to tell you this. The people who have taken responsibility to solve the problems in the continent will keep getting richer. Thecompanies who construct the bad roads will definitely get bigger.

The companies who manufacture our basic needs will have abundance of money. The earlier we realize this, the better for all of us.

The problems are there for us not against us. It is our shortcut out of poverty. It is our shortcut to prominence. If we will develop indigenous companies and stop making other countries richer, it will amaze all and sundry that the money in Africa at the moment is beyond imagination. The money that will come from solving these problems in Africa will be too much for this generation of ours and the coming generation to spend.

To borrow a famous quote from J. F. Kennedy:

«When written in Chinese, the word 'crisis' is composed of two characters. One represents danger and the other represents opportunity.»

Little wonder the Chinese companies now dominate the African construction sector, with a market share larger than those of France, Italy, and US combined. This strength of Chinese firms in Africa's construction sector has continued to grow over the past few years despite the global construction market taking a downturn in the aftermath of the credit crunch.

Revenues of construction companies in central and southern Africa grew by 31.7% to US$27.52bn in 2009. North Africa grew 30.8% to US$29.29bn. At the same time, the share of Chinese enterprises in the African market rose significantly from 26.9% in 2007 to 42.4% in 2008 and back to 36.6% in 2009.

Wherever problems exist, it's a wealthy place

Another country worthy of mention here is Japan. Japan is widely known as one of the most technologically advanced countries in the world, and that can surely be seen through its cars. Japanese car brands are an exquisite breed of amazing and beautiful vehicles that can be seen all over the world. They spread tremendously because of their ease of use, an interesting technology that is included in them, but also thanks to numerous other tiny aspects as well, such as body shape and fuel consumption.

In addition to meeting domestic demand, Japan invaded the foreign car markets and by the mid-1970s was exporting over 1.8 million cars per year. Perhaps the car that became most widely associated with Japanese cars was the Toyota Corolla which debuted in 1996.

Honda is also one of the largest car manufacturers in the world, Honda was founded back in 1946 and since then it has been active in the automotive, aviation and telematics industries. They create everything from automobiles to motorcycles, power equipment, robots, engines, aircrafts, solar cells to mountain bikes. Since they have such a long history, they are widely known as some of the best Japanese car brands in the world. Their main cars are the Insight, Civic, Fit, Accord, CR-Z, legends, CR-V and many others.

This list wouldn't be complete if I fail to mention Mazda. Mazda is a company founded in 1920 that has created everything from automobiles to light trucks and engines. They have created numerous types of vehicles, but the most popular ones are the ones driven each by every day by people all over the world. They create around 1 million cars per year, which is indeed amazing, to say the least.

As you can see, the Japanese car brands are some of the most popular ones in the world. Space will not permit me to mention other companies such as Nissan, Lexus, Mitsubishi and a host of others.

These companies that are meeting the world's demand for automobiles can only get richer. According to Forbes magazine, Toyota made sales of approximately $235.83 billion in 2016. Honda, on the other hand, has about 29,500 employees and made sales of about $118 billion US.

These car brands are popular cars in Africa and worldwide. A good percentage of the cars that ply our roads are imported, which means we contribute a large junk to the wealth of these companies. Now imagine how much we contribute to making other nations around the world richer, while we live in poverty.

These companies are only solving the problems of the demand for a means of transportation and they now smile to the bank. You too can smile to the bank if you pick a problem out there and decide to provide solutions to it.

Wherever there is a problem, there is money. Wherever problems exist, it's a wealthy place. When people see problems, begin to see solutions and that is your wealth.

Stop running away from your wealth

The irony is that everyone is looking for money but they are running away from problems. How can you be looking for money and you are running away from problems? I mean, look at Africa and other developing countries around the world. Most people are running away from developing countries. Most people are running away from what they call poor countries. They are running away from countries they perceive to have too many problems.

But in the real sense, those countries where people are poor, where there are so many problems, there lies the richest goldmines. While you are looking for ways to escape the so called 'problematic continent,' other nations are investing heavily in the continent and are looking for more problems to solve. This is simply because they understand the simple fact that where there is a problem, there is money.

The countries you want to run to have solved most of their problems and people have become rich throughthis. Meanwhile, your country is waiting for you to resolve her problems and become rich. You are only running away from your goldmine.

God placed you in Africa because He has a wealthy plan in place for you. His thoughts towards you are of good and not of evil. He placed you in a third world country because so much needs to be done. And if you avail yourself to be a part of the solution, you will enjoy your own share in the wealth of the land. If you will discipline yourself and work towards providing solutions to the problems in the land, your wealth will know no bound.

"There is no magic wand that can resolve our problems. The solution rests with our work and discipline."
-Jose Eduardo dos Santos

Wait a minute, think of the problems in the land. Come up with possible solutions to those problems and you will begin to see the business opportunities in these problems.

Every problem is a goldmine. The solution to any problem is wealth. The solution to any problem is money. The solution to any problem is a call to prominence. The solution to any problem is a call to significance. Therefore, stop running away from your wealth.

The government is not the solution. You are the solution. Don't wait for big opportunities. Start by solving small problems. Life has been conditioned to grow big things from small and insignificant things.

Microsoft started with two individuals. Facebook started with an individual in a dormitory. Google started exception. Big companies start with individuals. You are not an exception. You are here for such a time as this. You are a solution to your world. You are the solution they've been waiting for. Your wealth is tied to the problems you've decided to resolve.

My dear friend, there is no greener pasture anywhere. Wherever there is a problem, there is money. Your shortcut to prominence is problem. Your significance is tied to the problems you resolve. Your relevance in life is a product of the problems you solve. The more problems you resolve, the greater you become.

Lesson from Japan

The early cars built by Japanese companies were simply copies of American or European designed cars. Yamaha built Japan's first in-country produced bus in 1904 and the first domestically built car was built by Uchiyama in 1907. But Japan's real contribution to the automotive industry wouldn't come about until well after World War II (WWII).

In the 1920s and 1930s Ford, General Motors and Chrysler opened subsidiaries in Japan to produce cars for the Japanese market. Realizing their inability to compete directly with the Big Three in automobile manufacturing the government of Japan enacted the Automobile Manufacturing Industry Law to give the domestic car industry the upper-hand.

Following WWII Japan's auto industry continued basing its cars on designs originating with Europe and America, but eventually, in the 1960s, their automotive industry forged its own path. As the economy of Japan grew so did the consumer demand for cars and the Japanese auto industry turned from following to leading the world in design and in manufacturing innovation.

"Whether you're a farmer, builder or engineer, the opportunities are equal: Just add a little innovation"
– Strive Masiyiwa

The lesson I want you to pick from here is that we can turn from following to leading the world in any field we so choose to. The government of Japan might have enacted the Automobile Manufacturing Industry Law to give the domestic car industry the upper-hand, but if that is to be done in Africa now, where are the domestic companies that can meet the demands? Where are the indigenous companies that will be committed enough to solve the problems on the continent?

Complaining and giving negative reports like the ten spies have not and will not solve any problem. Stop the blame game and concentrate on solving problems. Focus on building businesses that will solve problems efficiently.

"Visionary people face the same problems everyone else faces; but rather than get paralyzed by their problems, visionaries immediately commit themselves to finding a solution."

-Bill Hybels

Every problem should birth a solution

With all the statistics given in this chapter of how much we spend on foreign companies and their products, will you now agree with me that there is money in Africa? Japan and China are just two examples of the countries taking advantage of the problems in Africa to get richer. There are a lot more but I believe you get the message I'm trying to pass across.

We lack good roads, they construct one for us. We need stadiums or complexes, their companies solve these problems for us. We need cars, they provide one. And they do all this at a price, which makes them bigger due to the high demand. You cannot stop them as long as they keep solving these problems.

Therefore, it's high time we stood up to this challenge. These problems exist because that's our shortcut to wealth. Let's therefore, begin to take advantage of the problems in our society, in our nations and around the world by providing solutions.

We lack good roads, they construct one for us. We need stadiums or complexes, their companies solve these problems for us. We need cars, they provide one. And they do all this at a price, which makes them bigger due to the high demand. You cannot stop them as long as they keep solving these problems.

Therefore, it's high time we stood up to this challenge. These problems exist because that's our shortcut to wealth. Let's therefore, begin to take advantage of the problems in our society, in our nations and around the world by providing solutions.

"Believe it can be done. When you believe something can be done, really believe, your mind will find the ways to do it. Believing a solution paves the way to a solution."
-David Joseph Schwartz

Every problem should birth a solution and the solution will bring the money. In the next chapter, I will show you how to practically turn problems into real cash. A problem is a call to business. Where there is a problem, there is money.

Nuggets

1. The irony of everything is the fact that while Africans are complaining there is no money in the continent, foreign companies who recognize the relationship between problems and money are making millions of dollars.

2. I don't need to be a prophet to tell you this. The people who have taken responsibility to solve the problems in the continent will keep getting richer. The companies who construct the bad roads will definitely get bigger. The companies who manufacture our basic needs will have an abundance of money. The earlier we realize this, the better for all of us.

3. The problems are there for us not against us. It is our shortcut out of poverty. It is our shortcut to prominence.

4. The government is not the solution. You are the solution. Don't wait for big opportunities. Start by solving small problems. Life has been conditioned to grow big things from small and insignificant things.

5. Your wealth is tied to the problems you've decided to resolve.

6. Stop the blame game and concentrate on solving problems. Focus on building businesses that will solve problems efficiently.

7. Every problem should birth a solution and the solution will bring the money.

8. A problem is a call to business.

CHAPTER 4

Can Everyone Become Rich?

Can Everyone Become Rich?

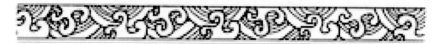

I once asked myself this question, Can everyone become rich? And I'm glad that today I have the answer. With no iota of doubt, I can emphatically tell you, "Yes," everyone can become rich.

What a person must do to become rich is not that hard. In fact, getting rich is easy, especially when you live in an environment with all sorts of problems. But most people would rather do things the hard way. Many will work hard all their lives living below their means, work hard for the rich rather work hard to solve pressing problems in the society and do what everyone else is doing rather than focus on coming up with solutions.

The first few chapters of this book have been primarily about those who have taken advantage and are still taking advantage of the problems they see to make them become richer. It has been about the people who have the eyes for problems and come up with an efficient solution. Meanwhile, this chapter and a couple of chapters following will be about what anyone can do and should do in order to turn problems into real cash.

There are many books written on how to become rich and never worry about money again. The problem with many of them is that they tell you to do things that are often too hard for most people to do. And at times, they are not realistic for the average person on the street.

This chapter is about the simple things that almost anybody can do. After reading this chapter, you will know that you have the ability to become very, very rich if you want to. Or at the barest minimum, you will find one or two things you can do that will make you richer if you so choose to do them.

And I can promise you that by the time you are done with the whole book; you will be aggressively looking for problems to solve. I can assure you that you will become an employer and not an employee. And I can boldly tell you that while others are looking for jobs, you will be creating jobs. So let's get started.

Refuse to be defined by your Problems

«You don't drown by falling in the water; you drown by staying there.»
— Edwin Louis Cole

What I will be sharing with you in this chapter is about a lady who gave true meaning to the above quote. She refused to be defined by what she experienced. I'll like to start by telling you how she turned her problem to a business venture.

Instead of running away from the problem, she came up with a solution and boom, a business was born. Her company has been featured on various local TV and radio stations as well as the BBC and CNN. She was motivated to start the company after her younger sister tragically died whilst traveling in Nigeria as a consequence of there being no medical air service available to transport her to the hospital.

Dr. Ola Orekunrin is a medical doctor, helicopter pilot, and the healthcare entrepreneur founder of Flying Doctors Nigeria, West Africa's first Air Ambulance Service. She's dedicated to bringing trauma care to the most remote parts of Western Africa and her company, an air ambulance service based in Lagos, is doing just that.

Ola graduated as a medical doctor from the University Of York in the UK and is a member of the American Academy of Aesthetic Medicine. Ola currently resides in Lagos, Nigeria where she is considered a national expert in disaster medicine and pre-hospital care.

The Turning Point

Ola Orekunrin's startup story is truly remarkable. She was originally born in London and grew up in a foster home with her sister in the small seaside town of Lowestoft in the south-east of England. With a passion for medicine, she studied at the University of York in the UK, graduating at the incredibly young age of 21 as a qualified doctor.

Her meteoric rise in the field of medical studies took her to Japan as a result of her being awarded the MEXT Japanese Government Scholarship. There, she conducted clinical research in the field of regenerative medicine at the Jikei University Hospital.

However, the catalyst for a major life and career decision came when her sister became very, very ill on holiday whilst staying with relatives in Nigeria. The local hospital was unable to manage her sickle cell anemia condition, and as a result, Ola and her family started to search for an air ambulance so that she could be safely transported to a suitable medical facility in the country.

The tragedy for the family was that there were no air ambulances to be found, even though the search took them from Nigeria to Ghana, Sierra Leone and Cameroon, and across West Africa. The only one to be found was in South Africa, 5 hours away, but by the time the logistics had been arranged, Ola's sister had died of her condition.

The real tragedy is that she didn't die because her condition was unmanageable; she died of a condition that could have been managed with the right medicines in the cupboard of a highly efficient Accident and Emergency hospital ward - it was just a problem of access.

The death of her sister and the circumstances that caused it broke Ola's heart, so she left her job and took the decision to move to Nigeria where she could try to make a difference in the lives of other patients and improving healthcare in the country as a whole.

In her own words…

"I just think that we need to start thinking outside the box and be more confident in the concept of African innovation."

Problem turned Business

When I read this story for the first time, I pictured what most people would have done. Remembered she was based outside the country, her younger sister only came for a holiday. I'm pretty sure most people would swear they will never visit the country again.

Most people would have complained and blamed the government like the ten spies did to Moses and Aaron. Most people would have run away from the problem they are meant to solve.

But let's take a closer look at how she responded to this problem.

She started to study evacuation models and air ambulance services in other developing countries before launching her ambitious entrepreneurial venture, Flying Doctors Nigeria Limited, which today enables her to combine her deep love for medicine and Africa with her growing passion for flying.

Ola is also a trainee helicopter pilot. Ultimately, her motivation for starting the business was to find an effective way of facilitating people who were critically ill, getting them to see the right doctor at the right facility within the right time frame for that particular illness.

Today, her business, Flying Doctors Nigeria Limited is the first air ambulance service in West Africa to provide urgent helicopter, airplane ambulance, and evacuation services for critically injured people.

"Every problem has in it the seeds of its own solution. If you don't have any problems, you don't get any seeds."
-Norman Vincent Peale

Surprisingly, the business was born out of a tragic problem that happened in her family. But she had the right attitude to problems. Her response to this problem is worthy of emulation. She took responsibility to solve the problem. She is a perfect example of the Bata Shoe Company sales representative. She is a Caleb and Joshua to the emergency medicine sector in the country. She brought hope to dying patients and now giving dying patients a second chance to live. Thanks to the problem she decided to solve.

"A positive attitude causes a chain reaction of positive thoughts, events, and outcomes. It is a catalyst and it sparks extraordinary results."

-Wade Boggs

Dr. Ola had a positive attitude, this led to a chain reaction of positive thoughts and a determination to confront a problem head-on and eventually it sparked an extraordinary result – West Africa's first air ambulance.

My dear brothers and sisters, what problems have you decided to resolve with your life? What solutions will you devote your life to? What problem will you be known to have resolved?

What are you doing with your time? Are you devoting your time to complaining or finding solutions? Are you excellent at finding faults or finding answers? Listen carefully; if you are not part of the solution, you are most likely part of the problem.

Making a difference in the lives of Patients

According to Dr. Ola Orekunrin,

«Sub-Saharan Africa has the world's smallest number of motorized vehicles but the highest rate of road traffic fatalities, with Nigeria and South Africa leading the pack. Trauma has become a silent epidemic in Africa, an epidemic that will only spread as the economy grows. More and more Africans are buying cars and working in heavy and dangerous industries. At the same time, infrastructure is poor, safety laws lax, and cars badly maintained.»

This has led to starting the first West Africa's Air Ambulance Service, Flying Doctors Nigeria. This is the same problem that every other person before her had seen and ignored, complained, blamed the government or at worst did nothing about it. The solution to this same problem is saving lives today and making someone richer.

Also, in her narrative, «When I arrived in Nigeria, I decided to start an air ambulance, not just a specialist pediatric air ambulance that would cover Nigeria and West Africa. It took a huge amount of work to get started with a lot of mistakes and a lot of completely dead ends.»

However, Ola's persistence, hard work, and gritty determination paid off, and today her company is well-established, well respected, and has won the applause and admiration from around the business world and from across the medical profession.

Similarly, over the past few years, the honors and accolades for Ola's work have begun to flow, with the prestigious World Economic Forum recognizing her considerable achievements by naming her amongst its prestigious Young Global Leaders class of 2013, a group it describes as the best of today's leaders under the age of 40.

The business now has a mixed-pool of more than 20 aircraft that are used for different types of evacuation, and about 30 staffs all employed in different capacities and branches in three major cities in Nigeria. Importantly, since the launch of the business, hundreds of lives have been saved – not just in Nigeria, but across the African continent.

The Lagos-based company has so far airlifted around 500 patients, using a fleet of planes and helicopters to rapidly move injured workers and critically ill people from remote areas to hospitals. From patients with road traffic trauma, to bomb blast injuries to gunshot wounds, Ola and her company are helping to save lives by moving these patients safely, rapidly, and providing a high level of care en route."

«... we take pride in being the first Nigerian indigenous company to do this... We are training more people to go into the air ambulance sector and I think our paramedics now have a huge amount of management skills. I just think that we need to start thinking outside the box and be more confident in the concept of African innovation.»

On any level, Ola Orekunrin is an inspirational Lioness of Africa, making not just a difference to the lives of patients in Nigeria, but across Africa and the globe through her example. She is a successful woman entrepreneur and inspirational leader in a world that needs more like her.

"Our children may learn about the heroes of the past. Our task is to make ourselves the architects of the future."

-Jomo Kenyatta

She has made herself one of the architects of the future in Africa's emergency Medicare. And her mission for Flying Doctors? She hopes this is the beginning of a healthcare revolution across West Africa.

What are you doing with the problems around you?

Quite a good number of people are desperate for money. Everybody is looking for money, but they are looking for money through jobs alone. They have forgotten or they don't even know that the problems around them are goldmines that could yield a lot of money.

A positive attitude is among the most important factors that can help turn a problem around. Those with a positive attitude like Caleb and Joshua don't complain, put blame on others, find faults or panic during crises. They focus their time and energy into planning and coming up with a solution to overcome the problem.

Wherever there is a problem, there is money because every problem needs a solution. And anybody that finds the solution monopolizes that area of life.

If you are hungry, that is a problem. Now, imagine there are no fast foods or restaurants around. Similarly, if you need to go to school, that is a problem. If you truly want to be educated you will find money to pay for your education. The school that provides this education exchanges your problem of ignorance for money. If you need to travel, that is also a problem. Wherever there is a problem, there is always money. Therefore I summit to you today that there is more money in the land where there are more problems.

The greater the problem, the bigger the wealth, So Start Now!

«One thing is sure. We have to do something. We have to do the best we know how at the moment . . . ; If it doesn't turn out right, we can modify it as we go along.»
— Franklin D. Roosevelt

There are still a lot of problems to be solved around you and you have to start acting and taking advantage of them. The problem of hunger is still crying for people to mechanize Agriculture and make food available at affordable prices. The problem of ignorance is waiting for schools that will educate people. The problem of nakedness is still waiting for clothing lines to spring up.

The greater the problem, the bigger the wealth. Therefore, I summit to you today that there is more money in Africa than the western world simply because there are more problems waiting to be resolved.

"Our beliefs about what we are and what we can be, precisely determine what we can be"
-Anthony Robbins

In conclusion, I will like to repeat this to you, anyone can become rich. You can become anything you want to become. Beginning from where you are right now, all that is required of you is to recognize a problem and come up with a solution to it.

Recognizing a problem around you is one of the easiest things to do. Listen to what people complain about. Listen to their pains. Pay careful attention to what they hate and like. Then go ahead and educate yourself to be able to solve the problem effectively.

As a close, I'll like to leave you with this one question, CAN YOU BECOME RICH?

The answer to this question lies within you and what you do with the problems around you. It's a decision you have to take. No one can do this for you. Caleb and Joshua chose how they responded to the problem that faced their generation. The Bata Shoe Company made their choice to solve a problem that other shoe companies were running away from.

What will you do with the problems around you? Sit down and complain? Come on dear friend, problems are goldmines, they are the diamond in your closet, therefore, go ahead and come up with solutions to every single problem. You are the architect of your life.And always remember this that the greater the problem you solve for people, the greater the wealth, so start NOW!

Next chapter will elaborate more on this topic as a show you more practical ways in which people have turned problems around to favor them and what you can also do to turn your problems around in your favor.

As you open to the next chapter pay careful attention to the wisdom sandwiched in every sentence because they are pointers to the enormous opportunities at your disposal already. The wealth you've been looking for and praying for have been waiting for you to do something about the problems around you.

Nuggets

1. Many will work hard all their lives living below their means, work hard for the rich rather work hard to solve pressing problems in the society and do what everyone else is doing rather than focus on coming up with solutions.

2. None of us is immune to problems, or adversity. And the truth is, it's impossible to prevent.

3. We always have "opportunity" which arises from bad situations, if we are willing to learn from adversity and deal with it properly.

4. Because we cannot prevent bad situations from coming into life, it is imperative that we learn how to transform them into positive situations—turn life's lemons into lemonade.

5. A positive attitude is among the most important factors that can help turn a problem around.

6. Those with a positive attitude like Caleb and Joshua don't complain, put blame on others, find faults or panic during crises. They focus their time and energy into planning and coming up with a solution to overcome the problem.

7. The greater the problem, the bigger the wealth.

8. There is more money in Africa than the western world simply because there are more problems waiting to be resolved.

CHAPTER 5

Stop looking for jobs. Look for problems!

Stop looking for jobs. Look for problems!

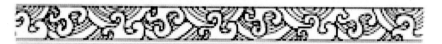

Can you imagine that in a lot of third world countries like Nigeria with a lot of problems, people are complaining about the lack of jobs? Young and talented graduates full of zeal and passion walk around the street with files from one office to another in search of jobs. This is because they are waiting for some other people or the government to solve the problems. They don't want to be the solution because it is far easier to put that responsibility on someone else.

"Responsibility: A detachable burden easily shifted to the shoulders of God, Fate, Fortune, Luck or one's neighbor. In the days of astrology, it was customary to unload it upon a star."

-Ambrose Bierce

They are perfect at analyzing the poor state of the nation's economy. They are very good at apportioning blames. They know everything that the leadership of their country is doing wrong. They know which state has the worst electricity supply. They know the number of accidents recorded on federal and state roads across the country. They recognize all the problems but one thing they've failed at is coming up with possible solutions to these problems.

And the reason why these people still go around looking for jobs and don't have any in places like Nigeria or South Africa, a country with one of the highest unemployment rate in the world right now is not because the country is bad. In fact, the bad state of the economy is a great opportunity for wealth creation. The more disorganized a country is, the better it is to make money in such systems.

Dr. Ola Orekunrin, the Bata Shoe Company, China, and Japan have all given true meaning to this statement that 'wherever there is a problem, there is a job.' They recognized a problem and created a niche for themselves. Very remarkable among them is the story of Flying Doctors Nigeria Ltd., started by Dr. Ola shortly after she lost her younger sister to a medical condition that could have been managed by an accessible and available emergency service.

Unfortunately, her younger sister died but that was the beginning of a new dawn for her. She became a CEO. She became an employer of labor instead of looking for jobs. After that incident, she can now live her life giving dying patients a second chance to live.In summary, the problem gave her a job. Wherever there is a problem, there is a job. Wherever there is a problem, there is money.

The simple reason why people look for jobs and don't find any is simply because they are not willing to be problem solvers. They are not willing to come up with solutions to problems.

Little wonder Henry Ford said;

"Thinking is the hardest work there is, which is probably the reason why so few engage in it."

This is absolutely true. We live in a world where very few are willing to sit down and think. They will rather go about apportioning blames. But Henry Ford knew better. He knew the power and potential hidden in his thoughts and that's why he came up with automobiles as a solution to the problem of transportation and has become the employer of those who has refused to use their mind to come up with solutions.

Go in search of Problems

Sadly, the wrong mindset you've been fed with is to go to school and graduate, then, look for a job. Did Henry Ford ever go around looking for jobs? Not really. Even if he did, he invested a considerable amount of time to think and come up with a solution to the problem of transportation. And that has made him an employer of labor instead of being an employee.

What of Dr. Ola of Flying Doctors? Instead of looking for jobs, she even left the one she had at hand to go in search of solving a pressing problem that has greater potential and could affect more lives. These are people who recognized the treasure hidden in an unresolved problem.

Similarly, China and Japan knew the potentials that are yet to be explored from the myriads of problems in Africa and that is why a lot of their companies are investing heavily in the continent.

"To succeed, jump as quickly at opportunities as you do at conclusions."

-Benjamin Franklin

Every unresolved problem is wealth. Every unresolved problem is an opportunity. Every unresolved problem is a job. You've got to wake up to this reality.

It is rather unfortunate that nobody ever told you or taught you to think in terms of being a problem solver. You are only looking for a readymade job. But you need a mind shift and a few biblical stories will help make this point clearer to you.

Listen my dear friend; you don't graduate to look for jobs. You are educated to identify problems and proffer solutions to such problems. Go in search of problems. Do extensive research and study on problems. Look for better ways to solve problems. Look for problems, don't look for jobs. Stop looking for jobs. Look for problems!

What else could have promoted a slave boy to prominence if not Problems?

Come to think of it, do you know how Joseph got a job? Do you know how he got a position of significance in one of the most developed countries in his days? Have you forgotten how he went from being a prisoner to political leadership? What else could have promoted a slave boy to prominence? Only problems of course!

The story of Joseph is found in the Book of Genesis, from Genesis 37 through Genesis 50. Joseph's saga is both expansive and integral to the overall narrative of the Israelites' descent into Egypt. His progression from dream-interpreting shepherd to the prime minister of Egypt is one of the more layered and elaborate stories in the Bible.

Joseph's life is a series of highs and lows — literally and figuratively. In his father's house, Joseph is the favored son. Israel (another name for Jacob) loved Joseph more than all his sons since he was a child of his old age.

Joseph likely also has this status because he is the eldest child of Jacob's favorite (deceased) wife, Rachel. To demonstrate this preference, Jacob gifts Joseph with the famous 'Coat of many colors.' This preferential treatment from their father elicits much jealousy from Joseph's 10 older brothers.

As a teenager, Joseph does little to ingratiate himself to his brothers. To find more favor with his father, he would report back unkindly about his older brothers' activities while tending to the flocks. Joseph also told his family about two dreams he had, the first in which 11 sheaves of wheat bow down to his, and a second where the sun, the moon, and 11 stars all bow to him as well. In each case, Joseph interprets the dream as meaning that one day he will rule over his family.

Eventually, the brothers act on their emotions. Seeing the "dreamer" approach on a shepherding trip, they ambushed Joseph and threw him into a pit — the first of the great depths to which Joseph will sink. The brothers soon sold him to the Midianites who in turn sold him to an Ishmaelite caravan headed down to Egypt, continuing Joseph's descent. The brothers then tore up Joseph's special coat, dipped it in goat's blood, and presented it to Jacob as proof of his son's death.

From Slavery to Prime Minister

And now, here is the account of the problem that got Joseph a job. Thanks to the fact that there was a dream no one in the land could interpret.

Joseph's time in Egypt is even more tumultuous than his life in Canaan. The Ishmaelite traders sold him as a slave to Potiphar, a wealthy Egyptian merchant. Joseph found great fortune with Potiphar, but his promotion through Potiphar's household attracts the attention of Potiphar's wife, who repeatedly tried to seduce him. When her attempts failed, she accused Joseph of rape, which landed him in prison.

Though now in the deepest of his life's trenches, God was still with Joseph. His fellow inmates, Pharaoh's former butler, and his former baker, both dreamt symbolic dreams, and Joseph's skills as a dream-interpreter were put to use. He predicted that the butler will be exonerated in three days and restored to Pharaoh's service and that the baker will be put to death. Joseph's interpretations came true.

Joseph asks the butler to remember him once he's back in Pharaoh's service, but the butler did not fulfill his promise until Pharaoh himself had a series of disturbing dreams two full years later. These dreams prove to be Joseph's ultimate turn of good luck.

He was brought to the court to interpret two famous dreams of Pharaoh: one in which seven sickly cows consume seven healthy cows, and a parallel dream in which seven sickly ears of grain consume seven lush ears of grain.

Joseph told Pharaoh: "Seven years are coming, a great abundance through the land. Then seven years of famine will arise." With this knowledge in hand, Pharaoh prepares Egypt for famine. Joseph, at the age of 30, is appointed second-in-command to Pharaoh.

"You will be in charge of my court, and all my people will take orders from you. Only I, sitting on my throne, will have a rank higher than yours. Pharaoh said to Joseph, "I hereby put you in charge of the entire land of Egypt."

Gen.
41:40-41 (NLT)

You might want to call this a miracle or anything you so wish to call it. But there is something here that I want you to take note of. It is the fact that even the so-called miracle was directed at solving a problem no one else could solve.

Joseph got his job as a foreigner on a Plata of Gold to be the second in command to one of the most powerful leaders in his generation, thanks to the problem he solved.

My dear friend, anywhere there is a problem, there is a job. Look for problems and once you identify the problems, begin to provide solutions. Once you see the problems, come up with your suggestions. Research on how best the problem can be resolved. Come up with calculated results. Come up with answers. Once you have an answer, that's the job.

The power hidden in resolving problems

There was a problem in Egypt. Nobody could give an answer to the problem but Joseph did. Joseph got his job because of the problem he resolved.

The famine that Joseph predicted ultimately brought the sons of Jacob to Egypt. With no other options, and hearing of excess grain in the neighboring country, Jacob's sons made a series of trips down to Egypt. Upon discovering his brothers some 20 years after selling him into slavery, Joseph concealed his identity and tested his family, locking up his brother Simeon until the rest of his brothers return with Benjamin.

Jacob was reluctant to send Benjamin — his last child of Rachel — but he ultimately relented. Only upon seeing Benjamin did Joseph revealed himself to his brothers, granted them forgiveness, and brought the entire family down to Egypt. Joseph died in Egypt at the age of 110.

You will notice here that Joseph's brothers came to Egypt to buy grains. That ultimately brings home this point again that where there is a problem, there is money.

The problem Joseph solved for Egypt got him the job quite alright but it also brought Egypt a fortune as one of the only countries in the world during that famine that had enough to eat and to sell to other nations. This same problem of famine that got Joseph a job also brought economic power to the nation of Egypt. This is the potential hidden in finding solutions to problems.

I can boldly tell you this that the hunger and poverty in Africa is one of the greatest wealth the continent is blessed with at the moment. If Egypt could turn a supposed problem – 'Famine' into a fortune, why can't Africa turn the hunger in the continent around in her favor to be a provider of food for the world? The solution to the numerous problems in Africa today could make her the leading continent tomorrow. These problems are waiting for you to solve them and make a fortune out of it. Are you still waiting around?

While a lot of people are complaining of lack of job opportunities in their indigenous countries, here comes Joseph, second-in-command in a foreign land in charge of their economic policies. That is a glaring model of the power hidden in resolving problems.

Finding a job is easy

Moses also got his calling because of a problem. While tending his father-in-law Jethro's sheep in the land of Midian, Moses saw a baffling sight on Mount Horeb. A bush was on fire, but it did not burn up. Moses went over to the burning bush to investigate, and the voice of God called to him.

God explained that he had seen how miserable his chosen people, the Hebrews, were in Egypt, where they were being held as slaves. God had come down from Heaven to rescue them. He picked Moses to carry out that task.

And that was it. Moses became a leader because of the problem God wanted to solve. He got a job. Not by going around looking for jobs but by being available and prepared to solve a problem.

Dear reader, finding a job is easy. Finding your financial freedom is also very easy. All you have to do is first look and see what God wants to be done, and then do what God wants done with the gifts that God has given you and the experiences He has allowed in your life.

If you will faithfully do that, the abundance of God will pour into your life. Life is not about earning a living. It is far more than that. Just look at the birds, the plants, and all of the nature's creations around you. Birds don't earn a living.

Birds and God's other creatures simply do what they were sent here to do. If you will simply trust in God and do what you were sent here to do which is to solve problems, God's abundance will be with you forever.

You don't have to do the bird's job. The bird is already doing it. This is because the world today is filled with a lot of people competing for jobs, rather than looking to see what problems are there to be solved. But I tell you this, if you will look to see what problem needs to be solved, and do what needs to be done to come up with a solution to the problem, then you will tap into God's abundance.

Take responsibility and run towards Problems

What of King David? Goliath was a problem to the children of God and David solved this problem. This was David's shortcut to prominence. The problem he solved brought him out of oblivion into a position of relevance and significance.

The Philistine army had gathered for war against Israel. The two armies faced each other, camped for battle on opposite sides of a steep valley. A Philistine giant measuring over nine feet tall and wearing full armor came out each day for forty days, mocking and challenging the Israelites to fight. His name was Goliath. Saul, the King of Israel, and the whole army were terrified of Goliath.

One day David, the youngest son of Jesse, was sent to the battle lines by his father to bring back news of his brothers. David was probably just a young teenager at the time. While there, David heard Goliath shouting his daily defiance, and he saw the great fear stirred within the men of Israel. David responded, «Who is this uncircumcised Philistine that he should defy the armies of God?»

So David volunteered to fight Goliath. It took some persuasion, but King Saul finally agreed to let David fight against the giant.

Dressed in his simple tunic, carrying his shepherd's staff, sling and a pouch full of stones, David approached Goliath. The giant cursed at him, hurling threats and insults.

David said to the Philistine, «You come against me with sword and spear and javelin, but I come against you in the name of the Lord Almighty, the God of the armies of Israel, whom you have defied ... today I will give the carcasses of the Philistine army to the birds of the air ... and the whole world will know that there is a God in Israel ... it is not by sword or spear that the Lord saves; for the battle is the Lord's, and he will give all of you into our hands.»

As Goliath moved in for the kill, David reached into his bag and slung one of his stones at Goliath's head. Finding a hole in the armor, the stone sank into the giant's forehead, and he fell face down on the ground.

This is the attitude that will open up God's abundance on you. The attitude that will take responsibility and run towards problems instead of running away from problems; this is the attitude that will make all problems fall face down on the ground.

If only you will be proactive today about the problems around you, you will discover that every problem has its solution within it like the hole in Goliath's armor. Every problem no matter how big and insurmountable it may appear to be has within it, its weakness and that's where the solution to the problem lies.

What problems will cease to exist because you are here on earth?

"It always seems impossible until it's done."

-Nelson Mandela

Come to think of it, if David had not moved closer to the problem, would he have discovered the hole in Goliath's armor? If David had not slung one of his stones would Goliath have fallen face down? That is to tell you that you'll need to sit down and think of the possible solutions to the problems. Do extensive research and study on the subject matter and come up with a solution. Then, and only then, will God's abundance come pouring down.

Finally, David took Goliath's sword, killed him and then cut off his head. When the Philistines saw that their hero was dead, they turned and ran. So the Israelites pursued, chasing and killing them and plundering their camp. So on that day David won a great victory and stood before all the land as the one who had saved his people from their enemies.

"Obstacles are like wild animals. They are cowards but they will bluff you if they can. If they see you are afraid of them… they are liable to spring upon you; but if you look them squarely in the eye, they will slink out of sight."

- Orison Swett Marden

You will be surprised as many so-called insurmountable problems will take to their heels if you will be dedicated enough to solve those problems. The problem of walking bare-footed in Africa took to its heels when Bata Shoe Company came to Africa. The Philistines took to their heels when David killed Goliath.

What problems will take to its heels because of you? What problems will cease to exist because you are here on earth? What businesses will you set up in answer to specific problems in your nation? Don't you tell me, you are still going about searching and competing for a high paying job when there are billions of dollars hidden in unresolved problems around you.

Everybody of significance that you admire got their job because there was a problem to be solved and they were equipped to be the solution. Anywhere you see a problem, there is a promotion. Joseph was elevated from prison to prime minister under 24 hours. Anywhere there is a problem, you got a business. Flying Doctors Nigeria Limited started by Dr. Ola Orekunrin is a business venture born out a tragic event. Anywhere there is a problem, you got a job. Moses got his job to lead the people of Israel out of slavery.

"I don't see the point of being a human being if you are not going to be responsible to your fellow human beings. Selfishness thefts away the human and reduces you to just a being."

-Terri Guillemets

Looking for jobs is just a selfish desire to earn you a living. Think and come up with solutions to problems that will affect other lives. Set up businesses to solve urgent issues that will give others a livelihood.

Stop looking for jobs, start looking for problems to solve for your nation. Start looking for problems to solve for your field. Start looking for problems to solve that will better the lives of people living in your community. It's time to arise!

Nuggets

1. The bad state of the economy is a great opportunity for wealth creation. The more disorganized a country is, the better it is to make money in such systems.

2. The simple reason why people look for jobs and don't find any is simply because they are not willing to be problem solvers.

3. Every unresolved problem is wealth. Every unresolved problem is an opportunity. Every unresolved problem is a job. You've got to wake up to this reality.

4. The hunger and poverty in Africa are one of the greatest wealth the continent is blessed with at the moment. The solution to the numerous problems in Africa today could make her the leading continent tomorrow.

5. Finding a job is easy. Finding your financial freedom is also very easy. All you have to do is first look and see what God wants to be done, and then do what God wants to be done with the gifts that God has given you and the experiences He has allowed in your life.

6. If you will simply trust in God and do what you were sent here to do which is to solve problems, God's abundance will be with you forever.

7. The world today is filled with a lot of people competing for jobs, rather than looking to see what problems are there to be solved.

8. Every problem no matter how big and insurmountable it may appear to be has within it its weakness and that's where the solution to the problem lies.

9. Everybody of significance that you admire got their job because there was a problem to be solved and they were equipped to be the solution.

CHAPTER 6

Don't worry about the Money

Don't worry about the Money

S ome people who have heard of my plans to go back to Nigeria have contacted me and asked me questions such as, 'do you think the government will give you money to do all those things you are talking about?'

But the government doesn't need to give me any money. God will give the wisdom and then wisdom gives the money. You only need to identify the problem.

God's wisdom in Joseph interpreted the dream, gave him a job and made Egypt an economic power house. The same wisdom enabled Moses to lead the children of Israel successfully out of Egypt and through the wilderness. Also, God's wisdom made Daniel indispensable in Babylon.

That is why the basis of discussion in the last chapter was for you to stop looking for jobs and start looking for problems. Don't go in search of jobs. Instead, look for answers. Look for solutions. Study the problems and come up with a solution.

Joseph had access to Pharaoh, the King, because of the answer he had. He did not go to Pharaoh with the intention of seeking for a job. He went to the palace with solutions and not with applications for jobs. And that solution made him the second-in-command in Egypt during one of the worst economic crisis those days.

My dear friends, if you can identify the problem and provide the solution, don't worry about the money. Never talk too much about money. Talk solution!

"First step in solving any problem is recognizing there is one."

–Aaron Sorkin

Whenever you identify the problem, thoroughly study the problem and the circumstances surrounding it, including other people who have resolved similar problems in other places. Then apply the principles they have used and advertise or publicize it that you've got what it takes to provide the solution. The money will come running.

In this chapter, I will be showing you examples of different innovators who just identified a problem, studied it and the circumstances surrounding it, including other people who have worked on similar projects before them. Then they applied the principles and the wisdom gotten from it to solve another problem and money came chasing after them.

Ask yourself questions

These innovators change things with the problems they solve. They take new ideas, sometimes their own, sometimes other people's, and develop and promote those ideas until they become an accepted part of our daily life.

Innovation requires self-confidence, a taste for taking calculated risks, leadership ability and a vision of what the future should be. Henry Ford had all these characteristics, but it took him many years to develop all of them fully.

It might interest you to know that Henry Ford did not invent the automobile. He didn't even invent the assembly line. But more than any other single individual, he was responsible for transforming the automobile from an invention of unknown utility into an innovation that profoundly shaped the 20th century and continues to affect our lives today.

There is a prophetic story of how the 13-year-old Henry Ford got a pocket watch for his birthday and then proceeded to take it apart. He simply wanted to know how it worked. It was a character trait that marked the rest of Ford's life. He wanted to know how things worked and, just as important, why they didn't work.

As you read along, it'll be very beneficial for you to take note of some of his subtle characteristics. Henry ford was a man that always wanted to know how things worked and when they didn't work, he also wanted to know why they didn't work. This quality of his to question things is very important if you are ever going to solve any significant problem in life. You've got to be inquisitive. Ask questions. Question the status quo.

"The questions we don't ask become the puzzles we don't solve."

–A. J. Darkholme

Ask why things worked the way they work. And be ever ready to learn. These qualities will lead you to a whole new world of possibilities and it will help you to have a new and innovative approach to problem resolution.

Ford was also interested in every aspect of life around him. He explored innovative forms of education which, in time, lead to the founding of the Edison Institute, known today as The Henry Ford.

In a single location, Ford brought together dozens of buildings and millions of artifacts. It was one of the largest collections of its kind ever assembled, as well as a bold and ambitious new way for people of all ages to discover and explore the richness of the American experience for themselves.

Henry Ford took inspiration from the past, saw opportunities for the future, and believed in technology as a force for improving people's lives. To him, technology wasn't just a source of profits, it was a way to harness new ideas and, innovatively, solve life's problems.

Work is an opportunity to learn new ways to solve more problems

His beginnings were perfectly ordinary. He was born on his father's farm in what is now Dearborn, Michigan on July 30, 1863. Early on Ford demonstrated some of the characteristics that would make him successful, powerful, and famous and a prolific problem solver of his days.

He organized other boys to build rudimentary water wheels and steam engines. He learned about full-sized steam engines by becoming friends with the men who ran them. He taught himself to fix watches and used the watches as textbooks to learn the rudiments of machine design. Thus, young Ford demonstrated a voracious curiosity, a mechanical ability, a facility for leadership, and a preference for learning by trial-and-error. These characteristics would become the foundation of his whole career.

Ford could have followed in his father's footsteps and become a farmer. But young Henry was fascinated by machines and was willing to take risks to pursue that fascination. In 1879 he left the farm to become an apprentice at the Michigan Car Company, a manufacturer of railroad cars in Detroit. Over the next two-and-one-half years he held several similar jobs, sometimes moving when he thought he could learn more somewhere else.

He returned home in 1882 but did a little farming. Instead, he operated and serviced portable steam engines used by farmers, occasionally worked in factories in

Detroit, and cut and sold timber from 40 acres of his father's land.

By now Ford was demonstrating another characteristic—a preference for working on his own rather than for somebody else. He was more concerned about the problems he could solve and how to make such solutions improve the lives of those around him. He was not selfishly thinking of how to earn a living all by himself. Even when he had to work, it was an opportunity to learn new ways to solve more problems.

In 1888 Ford married Clara Bryant and in 1891 they moved to Detroit where Henry had taken a job as night engineer for the Edison Electric Illuminating Company. Ford did not know a great deal about electricity. He saw the job in part as an opportunity to learn.

Henry was an apt pupil, and by 1896 had risen to chief engineer of the Illuminating Company. But he had other interests. He became one of the scores of people working in barns and small shops across the country trying to build horseless carriages.

Aided by a team of friends, his experiments culminated in 1896 with the completion of his first self-propelled vehicle, the Quadricycle. It had four wire wheels that looked like heavy bicycle wheels, was steered with a tiller like a boat, and had only two forward speeds with no reverse.

"The intelligent man is one who has successfully fulfilled many accomplishments, and is yet willing to learn more."

–Ed Parker

Ford's qualities of learning new ways to improve on the old means of transportation gave birth to the first vehicle. In the process, he took a job for the sole purpose of improving his skills. He even changed jobs for an opportunity to learn new things.

He is one of the greatest innovators of the 20th century because he always asks questions. He questions the status quo. He sought for new and better ways to move from one place to another. My dear friend, these characteristics are some of the greatest secrets of solving problems.

If you were to be asked, I'm pretty sure that the main reason why a lot of people will change their job is simply because it has a higher pay. Not because it could afford them new opportunities to learn and become better at managing the problems around them.

But just stay with me and I'll show you how much fortune could come out of solving problems as compared to seeking for high paying jobs.

No problem can be solved from the same level of consciousness that created it

This was a quote by one of the best brains to ever grace this planet.

"No problem can be solved from the same level of consciousness that created it."
-Albert Einstein

Just as Albert Einstein rightly said here, I guessed this was what pushed Henry Ford to keep questioning how to improve on the old means of transportation.

He asked questions. He questions the status quo. He asked why things worked. He also asked why things didn't work. He changed jobs for a new learning experience. He was curious about coming up with new ways to do things. And all these have led to the development of the automobile industry.

Henry Ford realized that he needed another level of consciousness to be able to come up with solutions and that's what he did by always learning. If a problem has long existed, it is simply because no one has changed their level of consciousness to be able to think at a level that will solve such problems.

Dr. Ola Orekunrin changed her level of consciousness about the problem of emergency care on the continent and it birthed Flying Doctors. Bata Shoe Company did the same. Japan and China did the same about the problems in the African continent. Caleb, Joshua, David, Joseph, Moses and a host of others have also operated at a different level of consciousness higher than the level of consciousness that created the problem to be able to come up with solutions and a mindset that solved the problem. This also has not only helped to come up with the quadricycle, it has birthed the second car.

The second car followed in 1898. Ford now demonstrated one of the keys to his future success—the ability to articulate a vision and convince other people to sign on and help him achieve that vision. He persuaded a group of businessmen to back him in the biggest risk of his life—a company to make and sell horseless carriages.

But Ford knew nothing about running a business, and learning by trial-and-error always involves failure. The new company failed, as did a second. To revive his fortunes Ford took bigger risks, building and even driving racing cars. The success of these cars attracted additional financial backers, and on June 16, 1903, Henry incorporated his third automotive venture, Ford Motor Company.

The Birth of Ford Motor Company

The early history of Ford Motor Company illustrates one of Henry Ford's most important talents—an ability to identify and attract outstanding people. He hired a core of young, able men who believed in his vision and would make Ford Motor Company into one of the world's great industrial enterprises.

The new company's first car, called the Model A, was followed by a variety of improved models. In 1907 Ford's four-cylinder, $600 Model N became the best-selling car in the country. But by this time Ford had a bigger vision: a better, cheaper "motorcar for the great multitude." Ford was dedicated to the production of an efficient and reliable automobile that would be affordable for everyone. Working with a hand-picked group of employees he came up with the Model T, introduced on October 1, 1908.

The Model T was easy to operate, maintain, and handle on rough roads. It immediately became a huge success. Ford could easily sell all he could make, but he wanted to make all he could sell. Doing that required a bigger factory.

In 1910 the company moved into a huge new plant in Highland Park, Michigan, just north of Detroit. There Ford Motor Company began a relentless drive to increase production and lower costs. Henry and his team borrowed concepts from watch makers, gun makers, bicycle makers, and meat packers, mixed them with their own ideas and by late 1913 they had developed a moving assembly line for automobiles. Turnover was so high that the company had to hire 53,000 people a year.

In order to meet the overwhelming demand for the revolutionary vehicle, Ford introduced revolutionary new mass-production methods, including large production plants, the use of standardized, interchangeable parts and, in 1913, the world's first moving assembly line for cars. The mass production techniques Henry Ford championed eventually allowed Ford Motor Company to turn out one Model T every 24 seconds.

In 1914, Ford also increased the daily wage for an eight-hour day for his workers to $5 (up from $2.34 for nine hours), setting a standard for the industry. At a stroke, he stabilized his workforce and gave workers the ability to buy the very cars they made. Model T sales rose steadily as the price dropped. By 1922 half the cars in America were Model Ts and a new two-passenger runabout could be had for as little as $269.

The power of identifying a Problem

Henry Ford had laid the foundation of the twentieth century. The assembly line became the century's characteristic production mode, eventually applied to everything from phonographs to hamburgers.

High wage, low skilled factory jobs pioneered by Ford accelerated both immigration from overseas and the movement of Americans from the farms to the cities. The same jobs also accelerated the movement of the same people into an ever expanding middle class.

In a dramatic demonstration of the law of unintended consequences, the creation of huge numbers of low skilled workers gave rise in the 1930s to industrial unionism as a potent social and political force. The Model T spawned mass automobility, altering our living patterns, our leisure activities, our landscape, even our atmosphere.

"Most people spend more time and energy going around problems than in trying to solve them."
-Henry Ford

This is the story of one man who has forever changed the way we move from one place to another. He dominated a nation's automobile industry during his early days. As if that wasn't enough, through this company, others could earn a livelihood. This innovation also helped other related industries to spring up just like Uber, which you will be reading about shortly. This is the power of identifying a problem and seeking for ways to come up with an efficient solution.

Ford, considered one of America's leading businessmen, is credited today for helping to build America's economy during the nation's vulnerable early years. His legacy will live on for decades to come. Ford was the creative force behind an industry of unprecedented size and wealth that in only a few decades permanently changed the economic

Ford's success in making the automobile a basic necessity turned out to be but a prelude to a more widespread revolution. The development of mass-production techniques, which enabled the company eventually to turn out a Model T every 24 seconds; the frequent reductions in the price of the car made possible by economies of scale; and the payment of a living wage that raised workers above subsistence and made them potential customers for, among other things, automobiles—these innovations changed the very structure of the society we live in today.

Listen to your own complains

Another interesting story I'll like to share with you in this chapter is the story of a start-up transport company. This story will give you deeper understandings when I say don't worry about money. All that is required of you is to identify a problem and brain storm on the most efficient solution to the problem.

The story of Uber takes us back to 2008 when the co-founders then, still friends and not aware they'll be at the head of one of the most successful startups up to date, were attending LeWeb conference in Paris. Travis Kalanick and Garrett Camp, like old pals, were complaining about the many crappy things we all have to deal with in life, including finding a cab when we're packed with luggage under the rain and no taxi seems to pass by.

These two "uber" kids were already brainstorming, thinking about ways to solve this global issue of finding cars at the right place, at the right time.

Garrett's big idea was cracking the horrible taxi problem in San Francisco — getting stranded on the streets of San Francisco is familiar territory for any San Franciscan. They resorted to using technology to exploit a gap in the market and scaling so quickly that it is now operating in 250 cities across 51 countries, backed by the likes of Google Ventures, and Fidelity Investments.

In 2010, Uber launched in San Francisco, providing full size luxury cars for hire, "UberBlacks," as they were then known. But they were also marketing themselves as a ride sharing Company to ease the pain of being unable to locate a cab on the streets of San Francisco.

"Business is all about solving people's problems - at a profit."

–Paul Marsden

As Uber launched around the world customers could now use their smartphones to find out where an Uber car was, how long they would have to wait, and roughly how much it would cost. And the problem of being stranded in a city at night, at times under the rain and no taxi seems to be passing gets solved.

Today Uber is one of the leading transportation services in the world and the company is valuedat $17 Billion US. This is the power of identifying a problem and brainstorming on the possible solutions.

Remember all they did was to listen to their own complains and the pains associated with finding a cab while at a conference in Paris, France and it led to a billion dollar company. This time around you are my witness; they never worried about the money. They only identified the problem and solved it. But when they solved the problem, the money came chasing after them.

"Focusing your life solely on making a buck shows a poverty of ambition. It asks too little of yourself. And it will leave you unfulfilled."
–Barack Obama

Don't look too far away

You might not have to even go as far as doing a market research on the pressing needs in order to start up a business. Listening to your pains, paying careful attention to your own problems, noticing what makes you uncomfortable at times is all that you need to start living in your millions and billions of dollars.

Problems are goldmines, my dear friend. Wherever there is a problem, there is money. Don't look too far away. There is abundance right beside you. There are jobs opportunities more than all of us can ever fill in the world.

Henry Ford started mass production of cars. Definitely, the cars need roads to ride on, that's an opportunity for construction companies like the Chinese firms in Africa.

The cars need maintenance, that's also an opportunity. And now another start-up still related to the transportation industry is operating in the billions in a couple of years of its inception.

Wake up my dear friend, there is more than enough money around you. Wherever there is a problem, there is money. Someone is eating too much, that's an opportunity for the nutritionist to consult. That's a potential customer to some other person running a gym. It's a very long chain of problems, solutions, and money.

If another person is not eating enough that could also be an opportunity for a medical doctor in case the patient is suffering from anorexia.

Wherever there is a problem, there is money. Wherever there is a problem, there is a job. Wherever there is a problem, there is an opportunity.

"Success is a learnable skill. You can learn to succeed at anything. If you want to be a great golfer, you can learn how to do it. If you want to be a great piano player, you can learn how to do it. If you want to be truly happy, you can learn how to do it. If you want to be rich, you can learn how to do it. It doesn't matter where you are right now. It doesn't matter where you're starting from. What matters is that you are willing to learn."

–T. Hary Eker

Therefore never worry about the money; be willing to learn how to be better at solving problems and the money will take care of itself. Money is just a by-product of the problems you solve.

Nuggets

1. God will give the wisdom and then wisdom gives the money. You only need to identify the problem.

2. If you can identify the problem and provide the solution, don't worry about the money.

3. Ask why things worked the way they work. And be ever ready to learn. These qualities will lead you to a whole new world of possibilities and it will help you to have a new and innovative approach to problem resolution.

4. If a problem has long existed, it is simply because no one has changed their level of consciousness to be able to think at a level that will solve such problems.

5. You might not have to even go as far as doing a market research on the pressing needs in order to start up a business. Listening to your pains, paying careful attention to your own problems, noticing what makes you uncomfortable at times is all that you need to start living in your millions and billions of dollars.

6. There is more than enough money around you.

CHAPTER 7

Improve on the existing Products

Improve on the existing Products

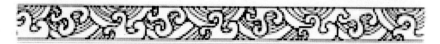

Just like the stories I've shared with you so far in the previous chapters, you don't necessary have to do something completely new or something that no one has heard of before you can start making your money.

The secret that I've been revealing to you so far is just about what anyone can do to become rich. It's what the rich have been doing to become richer. It's about the right attitude that seeks to solve problems. It's about looking around you to see what people complain about, the pain they experience, what causes them discomfort or what you can improve on.

It's the simple things anybody can do. And that's the reason why I told you earlier on that anyone can become rich if you choose to. You are the architect of your future. The problems you solve will determine the money at your disposal. And the more people you are able to solve this problem for will also determine the amount of money in your bank account. If the numbers of people that are affected by the problem are much, then, the bigger the money that accrues from solving such problems.

As a matter of fact, most of those we celebrate around the world today just did these same simple things. Steve Jobs, Bill Gates, Thomas Edison, Henry Ford and so on.

They didn't quite invent something that did not exist before but took their time and talent into making what existed better. They only improved on the existing products.

For example, many people around the world accredit the discovery of the electric bulb to Thomas Edison while in reality, he never did! Surprised?

The electric bulb has been in existence for several years before Thomas Edison. The major problem was the fact that the version of electric bulb available then was unreliable, expensive and short-lived.

Thomas Edison's contribution to the Electric Bulb

Thomas Edison only carbonized a piece of sewing thread. Using this as a filament, he was able to produce a light bulb that lasted for thirteen and a half hours. And by bending the filament, he could make the lamp burn for over 100 hours. Eventually, Edison invented the bulb that could glow for more than 1200 hours.

The only thing he did was to improve on an existing invention or idea because before him other scientists like Joseph Wilson Swan, Sir Humphrey Davy, Warren de la Rue, and Frederick de Moleyns had all worked on the incandescent lamp.

You can now see that real invention or solving problems around you isn't just about doing something completely new or doing something no one has ever done before. Real invention is taking what already exists and taking it to the next level. It is about perfecting something that existed before. It's all about making it better.

In fact, historians estimated that over twenty inventors worked toward the creation and design of the light bulb. Of these, Edison's version was the most efficient. So, my dear friend, it's all about coming up with the most efficient way to solve problems and you will never have to worry about money again.

And as long as consumers have problems, they will always search for solutions. People will always look for better, faster and smarter ways to accomplish everyday tasks. And fortunately for entrepreneurs, there are still lots of rooms for improvements in existing products. That said, the biggest issue for most founders is finding these painful problems and matching them with the best solutions possible.

By creating a vacuum inside the electric bulb, finding the right filament to use, and running lower voltage through the bulb, Edison was able to achieve a light bulb that lasted for many hours. This was a substantial improvement and one that led to more improvements and design, to making the light bulb practical and economical for everyday use.

So what Thomas Edison really did was to find a way to reduce the cost by making them with cheaper but efficient filaments that also lasted long hours. And even after Edison, others have been contributing and will still contribute to improving the light source.

It's an ever ending chain of newer and better ways to get things done. The light bulbs as we all know it today is a result of much time and effort and quite a number of people who took up this responsibility to invest their time and effort in improving it have made their billions like the General Electric of Thomas Edison. Remember that the next time you flip on the switch.

Why do I tell you all these? It is to help you see that you can become rich if you so choose to. Edison only went on to improve on what others had discovered and made a difference that the world cannot forget him for.

What of Henry Ford? He did not invent the car. And even though he wasn't necessarily the originator of the idea, the truth remains that he made it possible for a larger number of people to drive a car by mass producing it. He also made it possible for the common man to have access to an automobile.

Think of Dr. Ola Orekunrin of Flying Doctors. She did not invent the helicopter or any of the medical equipment used in saving dying victims. She only made medical aid more accessible for emergency care. This is the same story for the Uber founders.

"Japan's very interesting. Some people think it copies things. I don't think that anymore. I think what they do is reinvent things. They will get something that's already been invented and study it until they thoroughly understand it. In some cases, they understand it better than the original inventor."

-Steve Jobs

Just think improvement, if that's all you can do.

Steve Jobs' contributions

In the same light, another prominent individual is the late Steve Jobs, former CEO, and Apple co-founder. Let's have a look on some of Steve Jobs' works which formed the tech-savvy environment we know of today. We'll kick off from the yesteryears going to the present.

The first in the line of his contributions would be the Apple II. Long before the affordable computer was born, and probably the tech-savvy generation were even born computers weren't that affordable for the regular person.

In fact, businesses can barely afford them. However, it was all thanks to Steve Jobs and Steve Wozniak that computers became affordable for home use when they founded Apple in 1976. Apple II was released a year later in 1977, the world's first mass-market personal computer. After that, the rest became history.

Computers had been around for decades before Jobs came onto the scene, but they were primarily expensive machines used for business purposes. Things began to change when Jobs and Steve Wozniak founded Apple Computers Inc. Dens, home offices, and schools around the world would never be the same.

If a modern tech-guru would have to take a peek at the Apple II, he may scoff at the outdated spec namely the 1-MHz processor and 4 KB RAM – a slow computer in today's standards. But would you believe that this changed everything and helped make everything what it is today?

When the Apple Macintosh exploded onto the market in 1984, it was billed as "The computer for the rest of us." The Macintosh really introduced the graphic-user interface to the world. A graphic user interface allows the user to open files and programs by clicking on icons or menu choices with a mouse. That really pointed personal computing in a new direction.

The second in the lineup may be the multitasking computer called Lisa. Many have considered Lisa as a failure because of her rather eye-popping cost; however, what made her stand out despite that failure? First, she was the pioneer computer in the market in the drive computing area as she can multitask. Think of it as the current MacBook's great, great grandmother.

Roll in to the last years of the 20th century and we find ourselves transitioning from the diskettes and floppy disks to the circular, storage devices we are highly familiar with right now – and that is the CD. The iMac, when it was released in 1998, paved the way for the modern digital era as it was the first to shift from disk-drives to CD-ROM.

Aside from that, the iMac was the first to be the internet-ready computer available. Plus it was the first out of the many models to be a stylish computer with its colored and curved edges.

The modern 21st Century

"Our goal is to make the best devices in the world, not to be the biggest. "

-Steve Jobs

As we move on through the years we find our gadgets becoming smaller, handier and easy to carry everywhere. Steve Jobs did not stop with computers but rather, he also did a bit of exploring and one could say he changed the face of music forever.

Before, cassettes and CD players were highly popular and highly coveted. Soon, we were introduced to the mp3 format which paved the way to mp3 players and here comes the new challenger – in the form of the iPod. Although it wasn't really the pioneer mp3 player, the iPod, until now, has shown its dominance as the music player of today's generation. Apple didn't invent the portable mp3 player, but the company developed a version so good that it came to dominate and define the field.

And when there is the iPod there is also its partner – the iTunes. If you've been an iPod user for quite a while you will know that the iPod can never function without its compadre program. iTunes is responsible for the importation of the songs to the handy little music device as well as play and organizes ones music and videos on their computer. Not only that, the iTunes was also responsible for making online music stores possible. Music was only a click away.

Soon after, Steve Jobs became another contender in another area, which is mobile phones. Mobile phones have become not only a highly coveted accessory but also a necessity as well. The first iPhone was released in 2007 and featured a whole new outlook when it comes to mobile phones. Look at where it is now.

"What we want to do is make a leapfrog product that is way smarter than any mobile device has ever been, and super-easy to use. This is what iPhone is. OK? So, we're going to reinvent the phone."
-Steve Jobs

Finally, the last contribution of Steve Jobs before his untimely passing changed the interface of computers ever since. With the demand for smaller, lighter and handier laptops he introduced the iPad in 2010 which was a tablet computer.

Steve Jobs had a term to his products: magical. Absurd as it may sound, it does have its own sense of logic. His contributions to the technological world are indeed magical as they helped pave the way to the modern 21ˢᵗ century.

Listen my dear friends; there are opportunities that God has given you in life in order to make things better and more efficient. All Steve Jobs did to the computer was making it handier and user friendly. That was all he needed to do and he died a billionaire. He only improved on the existing products.

"I was worth over a million dollars when I was 23. And over ten million dollars when I was 24, and over a hundred million dollars when I was 25. And you know what, it wasn't that important because I never did it for the money. I think money is a wonderful thing because it enables you to do things. It enables you to invest in ideas that don't have a short-term payback. At that time in my life, it was not the most important thing. The most important thing was the company, the people, the products we were making. And what we were going to enable people to do with these products. So I didn't think about the money a great deal. I never sold any stock. I just believed that the company would do very well over the long term."

This was Steve Jobs' words during The Lost Interview in 1995 in a 70 minute long interview.

If you will go all out looking for ways to make things better and more efficient, you will never have to worry about money again. When you see problems, think solution!

When you come across things that have been done in a particular way for a long time, think of ways to improve it. Never worry about money, solve problems, make things better, improve the existing products and services; and money will come chasing after you.

Just think improvement

I have found that oftentimes, people are of the opinion that for them to really make an impact in life, they have to get to the moon, find a way to live on mars or make some "out of the world" scientific discoveries! Yet, nothing can be farther from the truth than this. Steve Jobs and Thomas Edison have proven this.

Yes, there is the place of inventing something completely out of the world but that is not the only way to make a business out of problems. In most cases, we are better off starting by improving on what already exists. You are better off taking a clue from what is and making it better than it presently is.

You have developed skills and expertise in certain areas that can be used to bring about positive change. The exposures you have and the experiences you have gathered over the years were all for the same reason – making the world a better place. The circumstances surrounding the inception of Flying Doctors by Dr. Ola can attest to this fact.

"Creativity is just connecting things. When you ask creative people how they did something, they feel a little guilty because they didn't really do it, they just saw something. It seemed obvious to them after a while. That's because they were able to connect experiences they've had and synthesize new things."

-Steve Jobs

It's now time for you to put together all that you have acquired to make the products and services better in the areas you are passionate about. It is time you put your full weight into making sure that the area of society that God has brought you up for does not suffer again.

What makes you think you can't be the next person after Dr. Ola's Flying doctors to make medical care more affordable and accessible? You might be the sales representative that we need in the telecommunications industry. You might just be the Caleb and Joshua for our banking system.

Imagine a continent like Africa! Imagine that we all found our places and went all the way to make things better and improve on the existing products. Just imagine having the likes of Steve Jobs, Thomas Edison, and Dr. Ola in each sector of the economy, improving and innovatively solving pressing problems, thereby making the world a better place. Where would poverty be able to hide again in the continent?

So I will like to ask you, what is it in your field that you can improve on? What do you think you can make better for the benefit of the general public? Maybe, it is the sales or retail process that you can come up with a better idea. It can be the transportation problem or a tweak in the educational or political system that you can give birth to. Just think improvement!

Here are a couple pieces of insight to get you started.

Solve real painful problems:

Google made search better. Amazon simplified online buying and selling. Netflix solved on-demand streaming media. Uber is trying to make on-demand car service better. What can you make smarter or better?

What is the one painful problem you can solve without struggle? To grab your customer's attention, start by solving their needs, wants rarely make the cut. If your product is not a must-have, you could still find a way to repurpose it to solve a pressing need. If you have been able to identify a crucial problem that you can effectively execute and deliver to the market, you will be able to create a real business that matters.

Look for inefficiencies:

Computer Programmers tend to say they're the laziest people on the planet. They're always looking for an easier, more efficient way to do things. When you give a non-programmer and a programmer the same 10-hour task, the non-programmer will spend 10 hours doing the task manually. The programmer will spend 10 hours writing code to do the task with just the click of a button.

When Bill Gates sat down to write Microsoft BASIC in 1975, he was on edge the entire time, trying to make it faster and faster. He constantly looked for inefficiencies, maintaining that he wasn't "going to let that stuff creep in."

Similarly, you should always think critically about your business. There's always something that can be improved in terms of efficiency. The moment you stop searching for improvements is the moment your business becomes inefficient.

Your business should be your passion:

Some entrepreneurs look to solve problems they identify with or feel passionate. They choose this path because work because less about work and more about enjoying the journey.

You will need all the inspiration, commitment and the perseverance you can get to make it as an entrepreneur, hence the need to start a business you are passionate about.

«The happiest and most successful people I know don't just love what they do, they're obsessed with solving an important problem, something that matters to them,» Dropbox co-founder Drew Houston said this during the 2013 MIT commencement address.

Coupled with passion, is the ability to execute. If you can't deliver, you are not in business. Products with a real need are easy to market and you won't have to convince people about the existence of the problem and the need for your product because they identify with it.

You don't want to start a business that may not survive. Do your homework, validate your idea and make sure you have a real market for your idea. Don't just start another business; solve a real problem people actually have, to increase your chances of success.

"You have to be burning with 'An idea, or a problem, or a wrong that you want to right.' If you're not passionate enough from the start, you'll never stick it out."

– Steve Jobs

Asking the right questions:

Don't be afraid to ask questions. The right questions will help you determine the steps you need to take to tackle a major project. Clarifying the problem will help you identify a solution.

Focus on building a must have not a nice to have product:

Consumers are overwhelmed with the paradox of choice on daily basis. Attention spans are getting shorter in the age of multi-tasking and only a few products are getting noticed – with many being a solution for a 'must' not a 'want.' You need to be doing something different and better to make it in this world, as consumers expect and demand more than just another product. Therefore, let their problems matter to you.

Let the problems around you matter to you

The world lost one of the big giants of technology, namely Steve Jobs. He passed away on October 5, 2012, due to pancreatic cancer at the age of 56, however, that doesn't mean the world has lost his contributions, ideas and intangible influence in the development of the latest technological gadgets we are now enjoying today.

People come and people go, achievements and awards become a distant memory, however, contributions and legacies are often kept and honored forever. Steve Jobs and Thomas Edison are just two of the great heroes that helped make the world a better place in their lifetime. And we cannot deny that their influence will be felt for decades to come.

«Being the richest man in the cemetery doesn't matter to me ... Going to bed at night saying we've done something wonderful... that's what matters to me.»

-Steve Jobs

Let the problems around you matter to you and you will live the rest of your life in God's abundance.

Just think Improvement!

Nuggets

1. You don't necessary have to do something completely new or something that no one has heard of before you can start making your money.

2. If the numbers of people that are affected by the problem are much, then, the bigger the money that accrues from solving such problems.

3. Real invention is taking what already exists and taking it to the next level. It is about perfecting something that existed before. It's all about making it better.

4. If you will go all out looking for ways to make things better and more efficient, you will never have to worry about money again.

5. When you see problems, think solution! When you come across things that have been done in a particular way for a long time, think of ways to improve it.

6. Never worry about money, solve problems, make things better, improve the existing products and services; and money will come chasing after you.

7. Don't just start another business; solve a real problem people actually have, to increase your chances of success.

8. Let the problems around you matter to you and you will live the rest of your life in God's abundance.

CHAPTER 8

Don't just start another business; solve a real Problem

Don't just start another business; solve a real Problem

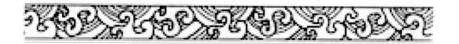

"The only people who make money work in a mint. The rest of us must 'earn' money. This is what causes those who keep looking for something for nothing or a free ride to fail in life. The only way to earn money is by providing people with services or products which are needed and useful."

-Earl Nightingale

This is an amazing quote from Earl Nightingale. The only way you are ever going to make a lasting source of revenue is by providing people with services or products which are needed and useful.

It's not enough to just improve on an existing product. It's not enough to just think improvement. It's not enough to stop looking for jobs. You need to start looking for real and painful problems to solve. The only way you are ever going to stop worrying about money is to solve real problems around you.

The only way you will ever become rich is to solve real problems around you. Take advantage of the existing problems. Confront the wrong mindset about problems and develop a positive approach to the problems in your society.

For you, this book may be about looking at old ideas and possibly finding new ideas for wealth. It may also be about a paradigm shift in your life. It may be about defining a new financial path for your life. It may also be about thinking more like a businessperson rather than an employee. But whatever business you might be involved in, make sure it is solving a real problem.

Save people money so they can live better

"Business is not about money. It's about making dreams come true for others and for you."

–Derek Sivers

In 1962, Sam Walton began a business journey that became the world's largest retailer and the biggest private employer, all behind one simple idea: *save people money so they can live better.* That was the simple problem he directed his business to solve.

Inspired by Walmart's entrepreneurial story, I looked into the life and lessons of its founder. If a humble man with a simple idea –everyday low costs- could become one of Time Magazine's world's most influential, why can't you?

Before the stores we know today, Sam had a small Ben Franklin franchise in Newport, Arkansas. Although inexperienced at retailing, he grew it profitably in less than five years only to lose it to a lease renewal mistake. Rather than regretting the loss, he saw that as an opportunity to start again – now with the experience. His next project, the commonly known Five-and-Dime in Bentonville, is what ultimately led to the first Walmart store nearby.

Sam Walton lived by discounts from the very start of his career. He said of one of his discount promotions, *«Here's the simple lesson we learned... By cutting your price you can boost your sales to a point where you can earn far more at a cheaper retail price than you would have by selling the item at a higher price. In retailer language, you can lower your mark- up but earn more because of increased volume.»*

"Every morning brings new potential, but if you dwell on the misfortunes of the day before, you tend to overlook tremendous opportunities."

-Harvey Mackay

Walton's strategy worked. He grew sales at Ben Franklin from $80,000 to $225,000 in just three years and was kicked out of his store location because his landlord wanted to give it to his son. So Walton moved on.

His next stop was Bentonville, Ark., where he opened Walton's Five and Dime under the Ben Franklin franchise. Before moving on to Walmart, Walton opened 14 of his small five and dime stores between 1951 and 1962.

Walton's model rested on a strong belief that discount stores could thrive in small towns, with populations of

Don't just start another business; solve a real Problem

5,000 or less, and if you sold products at the cheapest price possible, in turn, profits would rise. He proposed that Butler brothers of Ben Franklin cut their margins in half, and the brothers declined.

Sam decided to go it alone, and that's how Walmart was born. The very first Walmart opened in Rogers, Ark. in 1962. Walton and his wife Helen put up 95% of the money for the venture, but obviously, it has paid off. Before founder Sam Walton opened the discount store, he traveled the country, gathering ideas for everything he could do about discount retailing.

Save people money so they can live better - this was the simple problem Sam Walton decided to solve by starting a franchise. What problem is your business solving? Is it just about the profit? How will your business ease the pain and agony in your society?

If your business cannot answer any of the above questions, I guess you will be out of business soon. Money runs towards solutions. The problems you solve will determine the money that comes to you.

> **"Chase the vision, not the money; the money will end up following you."**
>
> -Tony Hsieh

155

A business that solves real problems will always grow

Just six years later Walmart began expanding outside of Arkansas state boarders. Walmart stores opened in two more southern states, Missouri and Oklahoma.

On October 31, 1969, Walmart was incorporated. In the spring of 1971, Walmart stock had its first 100% split and was sold at market price $47. By 1972, Walmart stock was traded on the New York Stock Exchange.

At this time the stock split 100% again, selling at $47.50. The store also continued expanding, staying in the south, with stores in Tennessee, Kentucky, and Mississippi.

In August of 1974, Walmart made its first acquisition, 16 Mohr Value Stores in Michigan and Illinois. Four years later, Walmart also acquired the Hutcheson Shoe Company.

By 1976, there were 18 Walmarts, and Walton closed all of his five and dimes, to focus all of his time, energy, and money on Walmart. As Walmart acquired other stores and expanded to more state (Illinois, the 10th state, 1977), it began transforming to the super store it is today.

In 1978, Walmart opened its pharmacy, auto service, and jewelry divisions. Walton's sell low strategy could be applied to any, and every, basic need product, because who wants to spend a fortune on prescriptions?

Celebrating its 18th birthday, Walmart became the fastest company to reach $1 billion in sales. The chain included were 276 stores, 21,000 associates,

$1.248 billion in sales. And in 1980 Walmart continued to expand across the United States. That is the power of taking a problem and solving it. If you are solving a real problem, your growth and expansion cannot be contested. Enormous opportunities and wealth will forever be tied to problems.

You need to constantly ask yourself how you will ease the stress and pain of people through the business you want to start. Like Sam Walton, what problem will your business be directed to solve?

What needs to be done? And what can I do?

With 1,198 stores, 200,000 associates, and $15.9 billion in sales, that is very impressive for a company at 25 years, which is still considerably young.

By the end of the decade, Walmarts were in over half of the states in the country. Small business owners fear Walmart's moving in to their town, but the truth is, Walmart neither hurt nor help small businesses. Walmarts are just another factor small businesses have to deal with.

In 1988, Walmart moved onto an even bigger project and opened its first supercenter. There has always been a resistance in towns when a Supercenter is said to move in, but somehow, Walmart seems to win. Initially, San Diego repealed an ordinance that strictly regulated the construction of Supercenters. Walmart now plans to build 12 Supercenters in the San Diego area.

I tell you this, my dear brother, a business that solves real problems is unstoppable and indispensable to their society. It's not about just thinking up ideas to start the next business, what problems will it solve? How will it make the lives of people better? If it's not going to solve a pressing problem, then why start it? Companies that run out of business are those that have lost their ideal of solving real problems.

By 1991, Walmart moved on to the international market, opening its first Walmart outside of U.S. lines in Mexico City, and the citizens of Mexico loved it. Just two years later, Walmart was doing so well in Mexico City, a supercenter opened as well.

In 1993, Walmart expanded to cover 49 states, every U.S. state except Vermont.

At the age of 74, in 1992, Walmart founder Sam Walton passed away. But just before Walton's passing, he received the Medal of Freedom, from President George H. W. Bush. This is an honor reserved for the nation's most respected civilians. The President said of Walton:

«An American original, Sam Walton embodies the entrepreneurial spirit and epitomizes the American dream. Concern for his employees, a commitment to his community and a desire to make a difference has been the hallmarks of his career.»

Walton's son, Robson Walton, was named the chairman of the board.

Finally, Walmart made it to cover 50 states with a Walmart opening in Vermont in 1995. At this point, the company had also acquired Woolco stores in Canada, opened value in Hong Kong, and opened a store in Argentina and Brazil. In 1996, Walmart even made its way to China.

In 1997 Walmart saw its first $100 billion sales year and became the largest private company in the United States. Just three years later, Walmart became the largest private employer in the world. Yet again, Sam Walton proves that if you will look to see what needs to be done, and do what needs to be done, you will tap into God's abundance.

Always question your mind in terms of what needs to be done? And what can I do?

Unsuccessful people live lives doing nothing, avoiding problems and also avoiding their wealth by default. It's very hard to ever get rich if you're going to be avoiding problems instead of solving real problems. A successful person, on the other hand, is one who is proactive in coming up with ways to solve real problems. And these successful ones are the people who set up successful businesses.

New problems call for new solutions

This was Sam Walton's way of getting rich by solving real problems in the society. Right now, I want you to fast forward to the present society we live in today.

During Sam Walton's days, Walmart had to build stores in any society they wanted to solve this problem. That is, if there is no Walmart store in a particular location, it also means 'no sales.' That is another problem right there. And solving this particular problem has made a lot of other individuals billionaires in U.S. dollars. But this will be discussed in detail in the next chapter. So don't stop here!

In this generation of ours, the main problem with Walmart's model is how to overcome geographical limitations. If you have a physical store, you are limited by the geographical area that you can service. But with an ecommerce website, the whole world is your playground. Additionally, the advent of mcommerce i.e., ecommerce on mobile devices, has dissolved every remaining limitation of geography.

"With the world now a global village, your vision has to transcend different races and faces in different places around the world."
–Onyi Anyado

Now, I believe you are beginning to see clearly that you can start by solving real problems, but never forget that you have to continually think improvement and innovation. While Sam Walton has made his billions in solving a particular problem, there are still a lot of problems crying for solutions. And these solutions are money making ventures. Therefore, I summit to you that wherever there is a problem there is an opportunity; wherever there is a problem, there is money.

At its core, e-commerce refers to the purchase and sale of goods and/or services via electronic channels such as the Internet. The medium grew with the increased availability of Internet access and the advent of popular online sellers in the 1990s and early 2000s.

Amazon began operating as a book-shipping business in Jeff Bezos' garage in 1995. EBay, which enables consumers to sell to each other online, introduced online auctions in 1995 and exploded with the 1997 Beanie Babies frenzy.

Like any digital technology or consumer-based purchasing market, e-commerce has evolved over the years. As mobile devices became more popular, mobile commerce has become its own market. With the rise of sites like Facebook and Pinterest, social media has become an important driver of e-commerce. As of 2014, Facebook drove 85 percent of social media-originating sales on e-commerce platform Shopify, according to Paymill.

The changing market represents a vast opportunity for businesses to improve their relevance and expand their market in the online world. By 2013, worldwide e-commerce sales reached $1.2 trillion, and U.S. mobile sales reached $38 billion, according to Statista. More than 40 percent of Internet users — 1 billion in total — have purchased goods online. These figures will continue to climb as mobile and Internet use expand both in the U.S. and in developing markets around the world.

This is the new problem that needs to be solved, which Walmart was not able to solve with its model. Overcoming geographical location; remain open 24 hours; Create targeted communication with the customer; provide abundant information about products and services and a lot of others.

When Walmart started, the internet was not so widespread, so he solved the problem the best way he could at that time. A couple of years later, things have changed and over a billion potential customers are online. This new problem calls for new solutions and those who provided the new solution are now living in their billions.

What are the new solutions that came with the Internet?

Overcome Geographical Limitations

If you have a physical store, you are limited by the geographical area that you can service. With an ecommerce website, the whole world is your playground. Additionally, the advent of mcommerce i.e., ecommerce on mobile devices, has dissolved every remaining limitation of geography.

Gain New Customers with Search Engine Visibility

Physical retail is driven by branding and relationships. In addition to these two drivers, online retail is also driven by traffic from search engines. It is not unusual for customers to follow a link in search engine results, and land up on an ecommerce website that they have never heard of. This additional source of traffic can be the tipping point for some ecommerce businesses.

Lower Costs

One of the most tangible positives of ecommerce is the lowered cost. A part of these lowered costs could be passed on to customers in the form of discounted prices. Here are some of the ways that costs can be reduced with ecommerce:

• Advertising and marketing: Organic search engine traffic, pay-per-click, and social media traffic are some of the advertising channels that can be cost-effective.

• The automation of checkout, billing, payments, inventory management, and other operational processes lowers the number of employees required to run an ecommerce setup.

• Real Estate: This one is a no-brainer. An ecommerce merchant does not need a prominent physical location.

Locate the Product Quicker

It is no longer about pushing a shopping cart to the correct aisle or scouting for the desired product. On an ecommerce website, customers can click through intuitive navigation or use a search box to immediately narrow down their product search. Some websites remember customer preferences and shopping lists to facilitate repeat purchase.

Eliminate Travel Time and Cost

It is not unusual for customers to travel long distances to reach their preferred physical store. Ecommerce allows them to visit the same store virtually, with a few mouse clicks.

Provide Comparison Shopping

Ecommerce facilitates comparison shopping. There are several online services that allow customers to browse multiple ecommerce merchants and find the best prices as compared to the hassle of moving from one store to another.

Provide Abundant Information

There are limitations to the amount of information that can be displayed in a physical store. It is difficult to equip employees to respond to customers who require information across product lines. Ecommerce websites can make additional information easily available to customers. Most of this information is provided by vendors and does not cost anything to create or maintain.

Create Targeted Communication

Using the information that a customer provides in the registration form, and by placing cookies on the customer's computer, an ecommerce merchant can access a lot of information about its customers. This, in turn, can be used to communicate relevant messages. An example: If you are searching for a certain product on Amazon.com, you will automatically be shown listings of other similar products. In addition, Amazon.com may also email you about related products.

Create Markets for Niche Products

Buyers and sellers of niche products can find it difficult to locate each other in the physical world. Online, it is only a matter of the customer searching for the product in a search engine. One example could be the purchase of obsolete parts. Instead of trashing older equipment for lack of spares, today we can locate parts online with great ease.

Sam Walton did not just start another company

In the next chapter, I will be sharing with you the stories of two men who took these new problems and solved them efficiently. Both men are now billionaires. They recognized the problem of geographical limitation, remaining open 24 hours without an additional cost, providing sufficient information about their products and services, the ease that comes with advertising and marketing online; and they came up with platforms that solved these problems.

Sam Walton did not just start another company; he solved a real problem then. Although things have changed right now; new problems are here that require new solutions and that's what you will be reading about in the next chapter.

The next chapter will be showing you examples of people who looked at the real problems in their generation and solved it. These are the people that recognized the opportunities hidden in problems. They are the people that have the right approach to problems.

They improved on the existing retail model. They did not create something completely new just like Steve Jobs of Apple Computers or Thomas Edison. They solved real problems with their businesses.

"The only people who make money work in a mint. The rest of us must 'earn' money. This is what causes those who keep looking for something for nothing or a free ride to fail in life. The only way to earn money is by providing people with services or products which are needed and useful."

-Earl Nightingale

I started this chapter with this quote and as I conclude I'll like you to read it again. Every one of us must earn money. Its way beyond starting another business, what real, useful, or painful problem is that business solving? Until you can answer this question, you have no business starting another company.

The rich will keep getting richer in as much as they are solving more problems and the poor will remain poor or get poorer if they will do nothing about the problems around them, wait for a free ride or keep looking to get something for nothing.

Nuggets

1. The only way you are ever going to make a lasting source of revenue is by providing people with services or products which are needed and useful.

2. Companies that run out of business are those that have lost their ideal of solving real problems.

3. Unsuccessful people live lives doing nothing, avoiding problems and also avoiding their wealth by default.

4. A successful person is one who is proactive in coming up with ways to solve real problems. And these successful ones are the people who set up successful businesses.

5. It's very hard to ever get rich if you're going to be avoiding problems instead of solving real problems.

6. You can start by solving real problems, but never forget that you have to continually think improvement and innovation.

7. While Sam Walton has made his billions in solving a particular problem; there are still a lot of problems crying for solutions. And these solutions are money making ventures. Therefore, I summit to you that wherever there is a problem there is money.

8. The rich will keep getting richer in as much as they are solving more problems and the poor will remain poor or get poorer if they will do nothing about the problems around them, wait for a free ride or keep looking to get something for nothing.

CHAPTER 9

Money runs towards Solutions

Money runs towards Solutions

In the last chapter, you read of how Sam Walton, the founder of Walmart solved a real problem of saving people money so they can live better through his franchise. In this chapter, I will be sharing with you stories of how some other individuals are solving another real problem of saving people the hassle and stress of retail marketing.

"The mint makes it first, it is up to you to make it last."
-Evan Esar

At the end of it all, it still boils down to one thing, money runs towards solutions. And it's your duty to find that solution. Whenever there is a solution to a pressing problem, money can never be scarce. Wherever there is a problem there is money.

If you can solve problems, you can be rich. If you have the right mindset about problems like Caleb and Joshua or King David and Joseph, you are unstoppable. And if you will turn bad situations around like Dr. Ola Orekunrin of Flying Doctors did, then, you are in for a very long ride in God's abundance.

I already gave you a preamble on how some individuals are already harnessing the potentials in ecommerce to solve the problem of overcoming geographical location and other limitations that come with retailing in physical stores. And in this chapter, I will elaborate more on that.

But just before you go ahead, think of this, if our maker has created a life of unlimited abundance, why should you plan on limiting yourself to having less? What do I mean by this statement?

If we live in a world with problems everywhere and new problems keep popping up every now and then, crying for solutions, why then will anyone choose to live from hand to mouth? When you've been taught and you now know that the solutions to these problems are goldmines waiting for you to have your share.

I will be introducing you to a couple of individuals in this chapter who are smart enough to know that God has created a life of abundance for everyone. All they did and all they ever needed to do to tap into that abundance was to look around for a problem and come up with an efficient solution to the problem.

The abundance in the world is enough to go round

Jeff Bezos, founder, and CEO of Amazon is one of the most powerful figures in the tech world today, with a net worth of roughly $57 billion. Today his «Everything Store» sells over $100 billion worth of goods a year.

Entrepreneur and e-commerce pioneer Jeff Bezos was born on January 12, 1964, in Albuquerque, New Mexico. Bezos had an early love of computers and studied computer science and electrical engineering at Princeton University. After graduation, he worked on Wall Street, and in 1990 he became the youngest senior vice president at the investment firm D.E. Shaw. Four years later, he quit his lucrative job to open Amazon.com, a virtual bookstore that became one of the internet's biggest success stories.

Bezos pursued his interest in computers at Princeton University, where he graduated *summa cum laude* in 1986 with a degree in computer science and electrical engineering. After graduation, he found work at several firms on Wall Street, including Fitel, Bankers Trust, and the investment firm D.E. Shaw. While his career in finance was extremely lucrative, Bezos chose to make a risky move into the nascent world of e-commerce. He quit his job in 1994, moved to Seattle and targeted the untapped potential of the internet market by opening an online bookstore.

If you paid careful attention here, you will discover that he quitted his job to solve a problem similar to what Dr. Ola Orekunrin of Flying Doctors did. People who recognize the potentials that come with problems can never end up earning a living through jobs, instead, they create jobs.

Little was heard or recorded about where he worked or what he earned before Amazon. But as soon as Amazon came into the picture, he has a net worth of $57 billion and sells well over $100 billion worth of goods annually.

Come on guys, what are you still waiting for? The abundance in the world is enough to go round my dear friend. Wake Up! Wake Up! Wake Up! There are thousand and one problems crying for solutions. The only reason why you are not yet experiencing that abundance is simply because you've not tasked yourself enough to come up with any solution to any problem.

"If you don't do it, nothing is possible. If you do it, at least, you have the hope that there's a chance."
–Jack Ma

Come up with more efficient solutions

Bezos set up the office for his fledgling company in his garage where, along with a few employees, he began developing software. The initial success of the company was meteoric. With no press promotion, Amazon.com sold books across the United States and in 45 foreign countries within 30 days. In two months, sales reached $20,000 a week, growing faster than Bezos and his start-up team had envisioned.

You will recall that it took Walmart more than 25 years to be able to have a store in every state in the Unites States of America. This is what Amazon achieved in a month and even sold books to foreign countries. Therefore, I can boldly tell you that the more efficient your solution is, the more growth your business will experience.

It's very good to come up with solutions but don't just start another business. It must be more effective in solving that particular problem. This was the secret of ecommerce. This is the advantage ecommerce had over the physical retail business.

Bezos continued to diversify Amazon's offerings with the sale of CDs and videos in 1998, and later clothes, electronics, toys and more through major retail partnerships. While many dot.coms of the early '90s went bust, Amazon flourished with yearly sales that jumped from $510,000 in 1995 to over $17 billion in 2011.

In 2007, the company released the Kindle, a handheld digital book reader that allowed users to buy, download, read and store their book selections.

In early December 2013, Bezos made headlines when he revealed a new, experimental initiative by Amazon, called «Amazon Prime Air,» using drones—remote-controlled machines that can perform an array of human tasks—to provide delivery services to customers. According to Bezos, these drones are able to carry items weighing up to five pounds and are capable of traveling within a 10-mile distance of the company's distribution center. He also stated that Prime Air could become a reality within as little as four or five years.

See the opportunities in Problems

Another prominent individual worthy of mention here is Jack Ma of Alibaba Group. Upon his first visit to the United States in 1995 as a translator, Jack Ma got introduced to the Internet, and to his shock after looking up a few products from various countries, he learned that there was none from China (a country of about a Billion people) on the World Wide Web.

"A pessimist sees the difficulty in every opportunity; an optimist sees the opportunity in every difficulty."

-Winston S. Churchill

Ma immediately saw the potential business opportunities of the internet and how it could facilitate the way small and medium Chinese enterprises could do business with the rest of the world. Then, he and his friends decided to launch a site about China and Chinese products online, known as "Chinapage", that listed Chinese businesses and their products.

The problem Jack Ma intended to use the internet and Alibaba to solve is to facilitate more globalized trade across borders beyond China and to help SMEs (Small and Medium Enterprises) across the world. Ma vows that helping SMEs to succeed is much like a religious calling for him.

Within the same day, "Chinapage" was launched, he began to receive emails from people around the world requesting that they partner up. That experience taught Ma about the incredible power of connectivity, especially how the internet can greatly impact global trade, particularly for SMEs.

Later, believing that «Chinapage» will get better funding, Ma partnered with a government entity that had majority control. Unfortunately, that entity brought along the rigid bureaucracy that stifled away many of Ma's visionary projects and frustrated him; which led to Ma's eventual departure.

In 1999, after leaving his government job, Ma took a second bite at internet-based business ventures by grouping 18 people (including himself and his wife) at his home and sold them a dream to found Alibaba with the goal of facilitating international trade for small and medium ventures based in China.

Jack Ma took the challenge upon himself to set up an online store for Chinese products. What problems are you solving for your nation? Dr. Ola of Flying Doctors set up an emergency Medicare for dying patients. What problem will cease to exist because you are around? David killed Goliath and saved a whole nation from humiliation. What problem are you going to address?

Like Caleb and Joshua believed against all odds that they were able to conquer and inherit the Promised Land, so are you supposed to approach every problem. Like King David killed Goliath, so are you supposed to solve every problem that is eating up your society.

Become a person that solves problems today. Be that person that sees opportunities in problems.

What gave birth to *'Alibaba?'*

Alibaba was born out of Ma's unfulfilled dream of using the internet to facilitate business activities for Chinese SMEs and frustration with the bureaucrats he worked with in the preceding joint venture (Chinapage), where his suggestions to use the internet to facilitate the trade of Chinese made products in the international market were repeatedly rejected.

In 2003, still unprofitable with Alibaba, Ma and his team launched an online auction site named "Taobao.com," charging zero commission, and took on a multinational e-commerce giant, eBay, which already had the lion share of the Chinese online auction market.

Determined to win against eBay, Taobao remained a commission-free marketplace for millions of online traders, and that did put Alibaba under significant financial strain. To stay afloat while maintaining the platform's commission-free policy, Ma and his team began offering peripheral value-added support services (e.g. custom webpages to online merchants) for small fees.

"In this world, if you want to win in the 21st century, you have to be making sure that making other people become powerful, empower others; making sure the other people are better than you are, then you will be successful."

–Jack Ma

Ma and his team won the Chinese market in less than five years, and eBay subsequently withdrew from China. Jack Ma reflected on this challenging period on a YouTube video of his interview with Charlie Rose, stating *"If eBay is the sharks in the Ocean, We (Alibaba and Taobao) are the crocodiles in the Yangtze River."* Since then, Alibaba has created many subsidiaries through organic growth (such as Tmall and AliExpress) and acquisitions.

The only reason why they were able to coerce eBay to withdraw from China is because they had a better approach to solve the problem at hand and the people valued them more. Your competition should be based on solving the problem more efficiently.

In 2014, in what turned out to be the largest initial public offering to date, Ma and his team successfully raised in excess of USD 20 Billion for Alibaba by listing it on the NYSE stock exchange in the United States. That made Alibaba, a 15 years old e-commerce company that has its origins outside of the United States, one of the world's largest companies as measured by its market capitalization that was approximately USD 200 Billion. Ma and his team are turning Alibaba holding group into a massive conglomerate by acquiring many smaller companies from technology related to logistics and beyond.

Jack Ma succeeded in one thing

The man known in the West as Jack Ma was born Ma Yun in 1964 in Hangzhou during China's Cultural Revolution. If few things can characterize Jack Ma's background, education, and the path to success, they are failures, rejections, fighting, resolve, hard work, agility, and vision. All throughout Jack Ma's life, from childhood till building a multibillion-dollar global ecommerce technology giant, he has failed many times, been rejected and called crazy, even by his father who warned him about his unique "dangerous" ideas that could have resulted in his imprisonment in an earlier generation.

Jack Ma has learned more from his and others' failures than through the traditional channels of education. Ma, a man of incredible resolve, has learned to fail better and fail forward. As he declared in an interview with Charlie Rose in Davos, «I failed a key primary school test 2 times, I failed the middle school test 3 times, I failed the college entrance exam 2 times and when I graduated, I was rejected for most jobs I applied for out of college." Ma was the only one out of 5 applicants to the police force to be rejected and the only one of 24 applicants to be a KFC manager to be rejected. «*I applied for Harvard ten times, got rejected ten times and I told myself that 'Someday I should go teach there.'*»

In the late 1990s after starting Alibaba, Ma tried to get venture capital funding in Silicon Valley for Alibaba and got rejected for running an unprofitable business model. He eventually went back to China without funding.

Like many brilliant innovative minds, both past and present, Ma struggled academically, especially throughout his early years in primary and secondary schools, where he failed repeatedly. However, he has succeeded in one thing. He has successfully excelled in solving a problem that has made him and a lot of others billionaires.

"The business schools teach a lot of skills about how to make money and how to run a business. But I want to tell people that if you want to run a business, you have to run the value first, to serve the others, to help the others – that's the key."

-Jack Ma

As an adolescent, he taught himself English and polished it by becoming an unofficial tour guide to foreign tourists. Through those tourists, pen pal relationships he cultivated with some of his tourist clients and his interaction with some relatives in Australia, Ma learned much about the outside world (especially the Western world). More importantly, he learned to question (not necessarily disbelieve) everything he thought or was told before, a practice he applies to this day.

That ability to question and reexamine issues helps him to look at situations from various angles and see opportunities where most see only problems. For example, when most people feared conducting e-commerce in China due to an unreliable and untrustworthy payment system, Ma got Alibaba to build Alipay without the Chinese banking authority's approval at the risk of his personal freedom. Now Alipay facilitates more business globally than PayPal, as measured in U.S. dollars.

According to the Bloomberg Billionaires Index Jack Ma is worth about $21.9 billion. With the help of more than a dozen friends who pooled their resources — just $60,000 — he founded Alibaba, a business-to-business online platform. The company now makes more profit than rivals Amazon.com and e-Bay combined, as China's burgeoning middle class are big spenders online, and small companies rely on Alibaba and its online payment system.

Ma is a charismatic, flamboyant and energetic leader, and his influence in business and leadership has been recognized by various organizations. He was named one of the world's most influential people by Time Magazine in 2009, businessperson of the year in 2007 by Business week, Asia's Heroes of Philanthropy in 2010 by Forbes Asia, one of 30 world's best CEOs by Barron's in 2008 and in 2001, he made the list of young global leaders by the World Economic Forum.

Educate yourself to be an expert in solving Problems

My dear friend, stop running away from challenges. Stop running away from problems. People who run away from problems lack understanding. People who run away from problems lack wisdom.

Had it been Jack Ma ignored the idea of creating an online business platform or did nothing about it the first time he saw the internet and he couldn't see any Chinese product online, where would he be today? Let's even talk about the millions of lives that have been affected by his site. Talk of the sellers that can now earn a livelihood. What about the ease of getting Chinese products across the world?

Listen carefully; you don't necessarily need to be an expert in that area. The wright brothers were not expert pilots. They went in search of knowledge and started something. They did their research and their homework. And the research brought them to the solution. They were more concerned about solving the problem than their limitations.

What about Henry Ford? That's the guy who popularized cars and dreamt of everybody having a car. Did you think he read mechanical engineering at the university? You think he was a graduate of Harvard? Maybe he attended Yale or Oxford University? No! A thousand times No! He was self-educated and burning with a desire to resolve a problem.

Talk of Thomas Edison and Steve Jobs, who both saw a need and researched on how best to meet the need. Did they study electrical engineering or computer engineering? That is if they ever saw the four walls of a school. Listen; if your education does not make you a problem solver, it is a waste.

Don't limit yourself to what you studied in school. Educate yourself to be an expert in problem resolution. If you see a problem, go on a research, dig deep and come up with a solution. Everything you see and enjoy today was born out of people who saw a problem and stayed awake to solve them. They added knowledge to their faith and the solution came.

"It's not that I'm so smart, it's just that I stay with problems longer."

-Albert Einstein

Finding Your Financial Freedom is Easy

You will notice that Jack Ma and Jeff Bezos did not repeat the same business model that Sam Walton of Walmart did. They looked for the next problem to solve. And it might interest you to know that there is always a problem to solve. They were not out there competing for jobs. In fact, they left the job they had at hand to solve a problem. They looked around to see what needed to be done and did it.

"Your big opportunity may be right where you are now."
-Napoleon Hill

If you will look around you to see what needs to be done, and do what needs to be done, you will certainly tap into God's abundance irrespective of your background, or race. Just look around for a problem to solve. By solving these problems you will discover that finding your own financial freedom is easy. And that's why I will repeat this again that everyone can become rich simply because there are so many problems crying for solutions around you. There are so many solutions crying for improvement and better ways to get things done. Right now, it's a matter of how rich do you wish to become?

"It is true that everyone has problems, and it is also true that every problem has a solution. If this is the reality of life, then why not focus on solutions rather than problems."
-Unknown

The interesting thing is every problem has a solution. Therefore, stop running away from problems. Stop being scared of problems. Stop being afraid of problems. Confront that wrong mindset you have about problems today.

Jeff Bezos of Amazon and Jack Ma of Alibaba group have proven that money runs towards solution. They have once again proven that wherever there is a problem, there is a job. If there is a job, there is a solution. If there is a solution, there is money. If there is money, there is fame. If there is fame, there is success. And if there is success, there is greatness.

Now, you can understand why I am going back to Africa because there are problems there. There are more problems there than Europe.

Nuggets

1. Whenever there is a solution to a pressing problem, money can never be scarce.

2. If our maker has created a life of unlimited abundance, why should you plan on limiting yourself to having less?

3. People who recognize the potentials that come with problems can never end up earning a living through jobs, instead, they create jobs.

4. Don't limit yourself to what you studied in school. Educate yourself to be an expert in problem resolution.

5. Everything you see and enjoy today was born out of people who saw a problem and stayed awake to solve them.

6. If you will look to see what needs to be done, and do what needs to be done, you will certainly tap into God's abundance irrespective of your background, or race.

CHAPTER 10

Every successful business is solving a Problem

Every successful business is solving a Problem

Many years ago in Nigeria, a country of about 100 million people only had two hundred thousand telephone (200,000) lines. Then the government thought of a policy to invite private companies in to resolve this problem. One of the companies that came in very early to address this demand was MTN. They were not very big in Africa then. But when they came in to resolve this problem, they are now one of the richest telecommunication companies in Africa, if not the first.

When they saw the problem, they knew it. And they came in to resolve it making them one of the biggest African companies on the continent. MTN is a South African company, so they didn't even have to look too far away. They saw a problem in Nigeria and came in to resolve it.

To the wise and people of understanding, they know that problem is their shortcut to wealth. The wise don't complain about problems, they make money out of problems. They set up businesses to solve those problems or meet pressing needs. They know that every successful business is solving a problem. They turn people's problem to their enterprise. They've come to realize that where there is a problem there is money.

"No enterprise can exist for itself alone. It ministers to some great need, it performs some great service, not for itself, but for others…or failing therein, it ceases to be profitable and ceases to exist."

– Calvin Coolidge

Nigeria's Telecom Journey

Telecommunications in Nigeria has come of age, even though it still faces challenges, which a thorough search would reveal, some are not peculiar to the country. Amidst these challenges, however, the telecom revolution in Africa's most populous country has recorded huge success as many would want to forget the unpalatable experiences of the pre-liberalization era.

As at independence, the control of Nigeria's telecommunications sector was vested in the Nigerian Post and Telecommunications (P&T) owned by the Federal Government. In the early 1980s, Nigerian External Telecommunications (NET) was formed to provide external communications services.

Following increased demand for the commercialization of telecommunications services, the Federal Government initiated the merger of NET with the telecommunications arm of P&T to form the Nigerian Telecommunications Limited (NITEL) in 1985.

From that period NITEL was saddled with the sole responsibility of meeting the telecommunications needs of Nigeria. Regrettably, it was unable to meet the growing demand for telecommunications services by Nigerians.

At independence, in 1960, the country had only 18,724 telephone lines. Up till 2001 when telecom was fully deregulated NITEL could not expand the installed capacity beyond 700,000 lines, thus limiting access to information and communications technology (ICT) in Nigeria. There were only 450,000 lines supposedly connected, with more than 50 per cent in federal and state government offices.

At that time, ICT was still in its infancy in Nigeria, knowledge, and use of computers was available to only a few people and they were either in multinational oil companies or a few government agencies and other large corporations.

The telephone subscriber base for telecommunications from 1985 when NITEL was established to 2001 when the industry was liberalized grew at an average rate of 10,000 lines yearly. The record was dismal for a country with huge population, abundant human and natural resources and huge prospect at independence. The situation was so bad that even with the reported 450,000 lines as of 1999; over 35 per cent were not functioning.

"Statistics suggest that when customers complain, business owners and managers ought to get excited about it. The complaining customer represents a huge opportunity for more business."

– Zig Ziglar

The problem in the country was the goldmine MTN came in to take advantage of. MTN grew from here to become one of the largest mobile telecommunication companies in Africa. This huge gap between those who had access to the mobile network as compared to the demand gave MTN the edge because they came in early to salvage the situation.

The populace decried the dismal state of the telecommunication industry in the country but that was a huge opportunity for MTN and the other companies that came in early to solve the problem.

Your shortcut to wealth and prominence

Between 1993 and 2001, the Nigerian Communications Commission (NCC) granted licenses to private companies to provide services such as fixed wireless telephony, mobile services and fixed satellite, paging, payphone, the internet and other value added services (VAS).

Before the auction, the NCC had carried out advertisements in the international media encouraging global players to come and open up the Nigerian telecom space. As far as the Nigerian regulator was concerned, the country was a bundle of opportunity, being the largest black nation deprived of mobile connection for several decades. It was an untapped market, so to speak.

But this was met with a barrage of cynicism with operators like Vodacom, which said it would never touch the Nigerian market even with a 10-metre pole. Many international mobile operating companies were afraid to invest in Nigeria despite the return to full democracy and establishment of transparent institutions like the NCC and other agencies to fight corruption.

In fact, international mobile operators were afraid to come to Nigerian just based on the reports by so-called experts and telecom research agencies and the global financial institutions like the World Bank and the International Monetary Fund (IMF), which had predicted that in the Nigerian telecom sector, the average Nigerian could not afford to own a mobile phone as the per capita income of the citizens was below the internationally recognized average. With this gloomy picture painted by the international community, the innumerable opportunities in the bustling country, Nigeria, were not seen.

Based on such reports, which clearly ignored or failed to acknowledge the special environment and nature of the people and the country, the telecom research agencies had forecasted that it would take a 12-month period for any operator to reach 100,000 subscribers, three years to connect 300,000 lines and five years to hit the half a million subscription mark.

This conservative report peddled to mobile operators about the market in Nigeria and other emerging markets put off many global players and investors that would have entered the auction at the time.

Let me take this opportunity to remind you of the story of Bata Shoe Company. Here is the point you need to read carefully. Bata Company sent their representative to survey Africa. Their representative was a lot smarter. He gave a report that Africans don't wear shoes. But he added that it will be a big market for his company if they take responsibility for providing shoes for all Africans. He advocated for his company to send people to educate the African populace about the need to wear shoes.

Two different sales representatives were sent to Africa, but they saw the problem differently. The problem of not putting on a shoe meant different things to these two individuals, just like the biblical story of Caleb, Joshua, and the other ten spies.

"Adopting the right attitude can convert a negative stress into a positive one."

-Hans Selye

Yet again, MTN is in the same position. And this is exactly what goes on between the successful businesses and the not so successful ones on a daily basis. How you respond to the problems around you will determine if the problem will work in your favor or against you.

MTN adopted the right attitude and the company soon became one of the biggest companies in Africa. They could now supply millions with mobile services. The problem they came in to solve was their shortcut to wealth and prominence.

The Next Time you see problems, that's Money

The course of Nigeria's telecom sector however changed in January 2001 with the auction which was globally adjudged to be a most transparent process. Thus, immediately, confidence began to build in the sector that had been feared to be a dead-on-arrival zone.

For instance, MTN's shares on the Johannesburg Stock Exchange fell sharply when news petered out that the company had won one of the licenses at the auction in Nigeria. Such were the initial cynicisms that would later give way when the companies all combined could hardly keep up with the pent up demand for mobile lines.

The auction and eventual licensing thus liberalized

the sector bringing in mobile operators like MTN, Econet (now Airtel), the comatose M-Tel); and further in 2003, Globacom to operate digital mobile phone services.

The telecom auction led to the revolution which liberalized and fired up a once sleepy sector, thereby striping NITEL of its monopoly and making the private telephone operators to reach out to Nigerians in droves. The success of the licensing process attracted international praise from all and sundry, including the International Telecommunication Union (ITU) and the Commonwealth Telecommunications Organization (CTO).

"The entrepreneur always searches for change, responds to it, and exploits it as an opportunity."

– Peter F. Drucker

The problem meant different things to different people. MTN and Airtel saw the problem as opportunities to be grabbed. When they saw the problems, they saw the money. They ran to solve the problems. And by solving these problems, they increased their wealth.

If you have to compete, compete to provide a better solution

With liberalization and emergence of private GSM operators, the ailing NITEL was also issued a mobile license to operate through its mobile arm M-Tel, thus becoming the third licensee after MTN and Econet. However, while the two other GSM operators launched in August 2001, it was not until 2002 that M-Tel launched following hiccups in the privatization of the national operator.

M-Tel at the height of its success as GSM service provider had about 200,000 subscribers which inadvertently plummeted as the crisis hit the mobile service provider under the watch of Transnational Corporation of Nigeria (Transcorp). Unfortunately, the same fate that befell its parent body would soon descend on M-Tel. For the second time, telecommunications under government failed Nigerians again and people continued to look up to the private GSM operators for mobile phone and allied valued added services.

With hopes dashed by NITEL and its mobile subsidiary, M-Tel, the government in its bid to rev up the sector soon coupled with pressure from the public given the runaway success being recorded by the only two operators at the time, MTN and Airtel, came up with the auction of a Second National Carrier License, which incidentally was won by an indigenous company, Globacom owned by business mogul, Otunba Mike Adenuga Jr.; the second richest man in Nigeria.

That led to the emergence of an indigenous telecom player, Globacom, which can today be described as the only National Carrier given the comatose status of the so called First National Carrier, NITEL and its mobile arm, M-Tel.

On august 29, 2003, precisely, Globacom joined the cast of the telecommunications business in Nigeria, rolling out its full service across the country. And that in a way helped to deepen competition among the operators, with the new entrant is throwing up competitive challenges against the older operators—MTN and Econet (Airtel) – especially with its per-second billing introduced right on arrival as the unique selling proposition. All other operators would sooner than later embraced the per-second billing, which they had previously given excuses about.

Therefore, those who look for solutions in times of crisis will always get richer no matter what the economy says. And that is exactly what those that are rich do. The economy doesn't dictate the money in your pocket, the problems you solve does. The rich get richer by solving the problems around them. The poor get poorer by doing nothing about the problems around them.

No problem solver will end up in Poverty

Today MTN has grown to be telecom services and business solutions provider, with mobile operations in nine African countries comprising South Africa, Nigeria, Cameroon, Cote d'lovire, Uganda, Botswana, Rwanda, Swaziland, and Zambia.

It conducts its mobile operations in Africa through three business units, namely MTN-SA (South Africa), MTN International (territories other than South Africa) and Strategic Investments. The group had 20.6 million mobile subscribers as on 30th September 2005, with 80 percent of the subscribers present in South Africa and Nigeria.

"Being able to touch so many people through my businesses, and make money while doing it, is a huge blessing."

– Magic Johnson

In the financial year 2005, the group reported revenues of USD 4.7 billion, an increase of 38.2 percent over the previous year. The increase in revenue was primarily due to strong performance in Nigeria and South Africa, boosted by the favorable economic environment in these markets.

Money is always connected to problems. Money is a by-product of problems. There is a cordial relationship between problems and money. Money and problems are relatives.

Together, the operations in South Africa and Nigeria accounted for 93.1 percent of the group's revenues. The revenue from data services has remained almost constant during 2004-2005, with non-voice services contributing only 3.9 percent in 2005 fractionally up from 3.6 percent in 2004.

All these shouldn't be a surprise for a company that saw a problem; looked for a way to solve the problem and then the solution has produced a corporation. The story of MTN Company once again attests to the fact that wherever there is a problem, there is money.

Every truly successful individual or business is solving a problem. No problem solver will end up in poverty. Where there is a problem, there is abundance of wealth.

Those that see problems as opportunities will always get richer

That is why a man like Carlos Slim from Mexico is one of the richest men in the world. As a matter of fact, he is the richest person in the world just a few years ago. I am referring to Mexico where a lot of people are running away from.

Carlos Slim is a Mexican born billionaire investor and famous philanthropist. He currently owns over 200 businesses in a wide variety of industries and has been named by 'Forbes' magazine, as the richest man in the world, several years in a row.

He learned basic business practices from his father, from a very early age, and worked in his family's business as a teenager. After he graduated from college, he began investing in earnest and slowly began building a multi-industry empire of conglomerates and corporations; both developed and purchased by him.

Today, he has holdings in Latin American and international companies, in industries ranging from construction and manufacturing to dry goods and tobacco. His most famous and influential holdings include his near complete monopoly over the mobile phone market, in Mexico, which at one point provided over 80% of the mobile services used in that country.

An inquisitive businessman, Slim has amassed a wide range of industries under his company 'Grupo Carso'. But his acquisition of the communications company 'Telmex' previously managed by the Mexican Government established his monopoly over the land phone and mobile services market as the company provided telecommunication services to about 80% of the Mexican population.

Every truly successful individual or business is solving a problem. No problem solver will end up in poverty. Wherever there is a problem, there is money, abundantly.

Those that see problems as opportunities, run towards the problem to solve it and create a business out of that solution will always get richer. While those who see problems as a bad omen, run away from problems and never think of a way to solve problems will always get poorer. It is a fact of life.

Between 2010 and 2013, 'Forbes' magazine ranked Slim as the richest man in the world, on their annual list of As of July 2016, his net worth was estimated at US$50 billion and he was ranked 7 on Forbes list of billionaires.

Money answers to problems my dear friend. Money follows problems. Money will chase you if you can come up with solutions to problems.

You are the determining factor

The shortage of mobile telecommunications in Nigeria meant different things to different companies. They saw the same problem but gave it different meanings. Their outlook and mindset on the same problem produced different results because they saw and interpreted the problem differently.

The sales representatives sent to survey Africa saw and knew that Africans don't wear shoes, but only one recognized the possibility buried in that problem. Similarly, MTN just like Caleb and Joshua discovered there was a shortage of mobile telecommunications supply in the most populous African country and told themselves *"We are well able to go up and solve this problem."* You know what? They actually did.

"The winners in life think constantly in terms of I can, I will, and I am. Losers, on the other hand, concentrate their waking thoughts on what they should have or would have done, or what they can't do."

– Dennis Waitley

Dear reader, the myriads of problems surrounding you is your shortcuts to wealth and abundance. The solution to these problems will bring you money than you can ever fathom.

My message to you today is that where there is a problem, there is money. Where there is a problem, there is a job waiting for you. Where there is a problem, there are enormous opportunities and possibilities. But you are the determining factor.

> *"The most practical, beautiful, workable philosophy in the world won't work - if you won't."*
>
> –Zig Ziglar

Your response and your attitude towards the problems around you will determine your experience. If the rich choose to be solving more problems, they will continue to get richer. And if the poor choose to be inactive and wait for some miracle, they will continue to get poorer. Problems are blessings in disguise. They are there for you.

Begin right now, to take advantage of the problems around you!

Nuggets

1. To the wise and people of understanding, they know that problem is their shortcut to wealth.

2. The wise don't complain about problems, they make money out of problems. They set up businesses to solve those problems or meet pressing needs. They know that every successful business is solving a problem. They turn people's problem to their enterprise. They've come to realize that where there is a problem there is money.

3. How you respond to the problems around you will determine if the problem will work in your favor or against you.

4. Those that look for solutions in times of crisis will always get richer no matter what the economy says.

5. The economy doesn't dictate the money in your pocket, the problems you solve does. The rich get richer by solving the problems around them. The poor get poorer by doing nothing about the problems around them.

6. Money is always connected to problems. Money is a by-product of problems.

7. Those that see problems as opportunities, run towards the problem to solve it and create a business out of that solution will always get richer. While those who see problems as a bad omen, run away from problems and never think of a way to solve problems will always get poorer. It is a fact of life.

8. Money answers to problems my dear friend. Money follows problems. Money will chase you if you can come up with solutions to problems.

CHAPTER 11

You are not needed without problems

You are not needed without problems

D o you know that without problems, you cannot be who you are? You are not needed without problems. You are useless without problems. Every one of us will not have any relevance or significance without solving one problem or the other. And I will give you a few examples in this chapter.

Imagine if you are a medical doctor, and no one is sick? Of what use is your profession and medical skills? As a cook, who cares how good you are in the kitchen if no one is hungry? You are only needed because somebody is hungry. Your culinary skill is only relevant because someone needs to eat.

Your provision is hidden in somebody's problem. So, why run away from problems? If not because of problems, you won't have a job. It is thanks to problem that you have a job. Why run away from problems then?

Thanks to the problem of sin, if not pastors like me will be useless. I tell you this that not a single one of us will be needed if we live in a world without problems.

If you are a lawyer, thank God for litigation. Thank God for crime and offence. So, if you are praying that we should live in a crime free society or you don't want anyone to get sick, what then happens to the lawyers and doctors?

"We are built to conquer our environment, solve problems, achieve goals, and we find no real satisfaction or happiness in life without obstacles to conquer and goals to achieve."

-Maxwell Malt

Therefore, I can boldly conclude that you are here for only one reason, which is to solve problems. You are actually not needed without problems to solve.

Just as every problem is an avenue for making money. If you are hungry, somebody makes money. If your car breaks down somebody makes money. If you are sick, someone is making money. As a matter of fact, when death comes, a lot of people will make more money. That's just how life is. The secret of life, therefore, is to look for problems to resolve. Be equipped to solve a problem. Stop complaining about problems. Instead, do extensive research on how to become an expert in solving problems.

Whenever you see problems, look for the best ways to resolve them. And when you solve problems for people that is an opportunity to excel in life. That also will bring favor, wealth, honor, and respect.

If you've been following my line of discussion, you will agree with me that money is not really the main deal. The main deal is our attitude to problems, how we respond to problems. The issue is the fact that you don't know how to relate to problems. And as soon as you get this right, you are in for a life of opportunities and possibilities.

You are as relevant as the problem you dedicate your life to solve

I will be showing you a few examples in this chapter of some individuals and I believe that by the time you are done reading through you will agree with me that they were and others are only relevant because of the problem they've dedicated their lives to solving.

Some of them you already know or you've read about them before. But I want you to pay careful attention to their stories and see how they were transformed from rags to riches, from mediocrity to prominence, all thanks to the problems they solved.

They are not people that ran away from problems. They had the right attitude to problems. They symbolize the 'Caleb and Joshua' to their industry and their generation. They don't hide from problems. They are problem solvers.

They run to problems like David did to Goliath. They approached problems the way Bata Shoe Company, MTN, China and Japan did when they saw problems in Africa. They are men and women of solutions. But the most important thing about their stories is the fact that without the problems they solved, you and I wouldn't have heard about them.

The Wright Brothers

The American aviation pioneers Wilbur and Orville Wright were the first to accomplish manned, powered flight in a heavier-than-air machine. Wilbur and Orville Wright were the sons of Milton Wright, a bishop of the United Brethren in Christ.

Their personalities were perfectly complementary (each provided what the other lacked). Orville was full of ideas and enthusiasms. Wilbur was steadier in his habits, more mature in his judgments, and more likely to see a project through.

In their early years, the two boys helped their father, who edited a journal called the *Religious Telescope*. Later, they began a paper of their own, *West Side News*. They went into business together as printers producing everything from religious handouts to commercial fliers. In 1892 they opened the Wright Cycle Shop in Dayton. This was the perfect occupation for the Wright brothers because it involved one of the exciting mechanical devices of the time: the bicycle. When the brothers took up the problems of flight, they had a solid grounding in practical mechanics (knowledge of how to build machines).

The exploits of one of the great glider pilots of the late nineteenth century, Otto Lilienthal, had attracted the attention of the Wright brothers as early as 1891, but it was not until the death of this famous aeronautical engineer in 1896 that the two became interested in gliding experiments.

They then decided to educate themselves in the theory and state of the art of flying.

The Wright brothers began by accumulating and mastering all the important information on the subject, designed and tested their own models and gliders, built their own engine, and, when the experimental data they had inherited appeared to be inadequate or wrong, they conducted new and more thorough experiments. The Wrights decided that earlier attempts at flight were not successful because the plans for early airplanes required pilots to shift their bodies to control the plane. The brothers decided that it would be better to control a plane by moving its wings.

The Wright brothers soon discovered, however, that no manufacturer would undertake to build an engine that would meet their specifications, so they had to build their own. They produced one that had four cylinders and developed 12 horsepower (a unit that describes the strength of an engine). When it was installed in the air frame, the entire machine weighed just 750 pounds and proved to be capable of traveling 31 miles per hour. They took this new airplane to Kitty Hawk in the fall of 1903 and on December 17 they made the world's first manned, powered flight in a heavier-than-air craft.

The first flight was made by Orville and lasted only 12 seconds, during which the airplane flew 120 feet. That same day, however, on its fourth flight, with Wilbur at the controls, the plane stayed in the air for 59 seconds and traveled 852 feet. Then a gust of wind severely damaged the craft. The brothers returned to Dayton convinced of their success and determined to build another machine. In 1905 they abandoned their other activities and concentrated on the development of aviation. On May 22, 1906, they received a patent for their flying machine.

Martin Luther King Jr.

He was one of the most prominent advocates of the Civil Rights movement during the 1960s. In contrast to some civil rights activists Martin Luther King generally promoted a non-violent strategy of social change.

Martin Luther King, Jr. was born in Atlanta on 15 January 1929. Both his father and grandfather were pastors in an African-American Baptist church, King would also later follow them into the ministry. It was at University that King became more aware of the civil rights struggle and he took the opportunity to study Mahatma Gandhi's non-violent strategy for social change.

A defining moment in the civil rights struggle was to a large degree instigated by Martin Luther King Jr. who was the president of the Montgomery Improvement Association. It began on 5 December 1955, when Rosa Parks a civil rights activist refused to given up her seat breaking the strict segregation on Montgomery's buses. King inspired black residents to launch a bus boycott which lasted well into 1956, this gained substantial media coverage and in December of the following year the United States Supreme

Court declared the segregation unconstitutional and the buses were desegregated. Following the success of this action, the civil rights movement gained strength.

Martin Luther King was one of the world's greatest orators. His deep and powerful voice was able to captivate audiences. His speeches caused him to become one of the most well-known civil rights leaders. In 1963 he was named as Time's man of the Year. It was in August of 1963 that King delivered his famous and iconic 'I have a Dream Speech.' The speech was given at the Lincoln Memorial in Washington D.C during the 250,000 march for civil rights.

At the age of thirty-five, Martin Luther King, Jr., was the youngest man to have received the Nobel Peace Prize (1964). When notified of his selection, he announced that he would turn over the prize money of $54,123 to the furtherance of the civil rights movement.

To this day, King remains a potent symbol of the African American civil rights movement. His speeches offer a striking exposition of some of the ideals of the civil rights movement.

The Courageous Queen Esther

The book of Esther is one of only two books in the entire Bible named for women. The other is the book of Ruth. Esther contains the story of a beautiful young Jewess who risked her life to serve God and save her people.

Esther lived in ancient Persia about 100 years after the Babylonian captivity. When Esther's parents died, the orphaned child was adopted and raised by her older cousin Mordecai.

One day the king of the Persian Empire, Xerxes I, threw a lavish party. On the final day of the festivities, he called for his queen, Vashti, eager to flaunt her beauty to his guests. But the queen refused to appear before Xerxes. Filled with anger, he deposed Queen Vashti, forever removing her from his presence.

To find his new queen, Xerxes hosted a royal beauty pageant and Esther was chosen for the throne. Her cousin Mordecai became a minor official in the Persian government of Susa.

Soon after, Mordecai uncovered a plot to assassinate the king. He told Esther about the conspiracy, and she reported it to Xerxes, giving credit to Mordecai. The plot was thwarted and Mordecai's act of kindness was preserved in the chronicles of the king.

At this same time, the king's highest official was a wicked man named Haman. He hated the Jews and he especially hated Mordecai, who had refused to bow down to him.

So, Haman devised a scheme to have every Jew in Persia killed. The king bought into the plot and agreed to annihilate the Jewish people on a specific day. Meanwhile,

Mordecai learned of the plan and shared it with Esther, challenging her with these famous words:

«Do not think that because you are in the king's house you alone of all the Jews will escape.
For if you remain silent at this time, relief and deliverance for the Jews will arise from another place, but you and your father's family will perish. And who knows but that you have come to your royal position for such a time as this?»

(Esther 4:13-14, NIV)

The Jewish exile Mordecai knew the situation was dire and dangerous. Esther and Mordecai knew that to come before the king without a formal invitation, even though Esther was the queen, could mean she would be put to death.

Esther urged all of the Jews to fast and pray for deliverance. Then risking her own life, brave young Esther approached the king with a plan of her own.

She invited Xerxes and Haman to a banquet where eventually she revealed her Jewish heritage to the king, as well as Haman's diabolical plot to have her and her people killed. In a rage, the king ordered Haman to be hung on the gallows--the very same gallows Haman had built for Mordecai.

Mordecai was promoted to Haman's high position and Jews were granted protection throughout the land. As the people celebrated God's tremendous deliverance, the joyous festival of Purim was instituted.

Nelson Mandela: the icon and the hero of African liberation

"We must use time wisely and forever realize that the time is always ripe to do right."

-Nelson Mandela

Nelson Mandela became known and respected all over the world as a symbol of the struggle against apartheid and all forms of racism; the icon and the hero of African liberation.

Mandela or Madiba, as he was affectionately known, has been called a freedom fighter, a great man, South Africa's Favorite Son, a global icon and a legend, among countless other names. He has been an activist, a political prisoner, South Africa's first democratically elected president, an international peacemaker and statesman, and a Nobel Peace Prize winner.

He is the most honored political prisoner in history; having served a prison term for 27 years from 1963 to 1990. But prison bars could not prevent him from continuing to inspire his people to struggle and sacrifice for their liberation.

«I have fought against white domination, and I have fought against black domination. I have cherished the ideal of a democratic and free society in which all persons live together in harmony and with equal opportunities. It is an ideal which I hope to live for and to achieve. But if needs be, it is an ideal for which I am prepared to die.»

-Nelson Mandela

In the winter of 1964, Nelson Mandela arrived on Robben Island where he would spend 18 of his 27 prison years. Confined to a small cell, the floor his bed, a bucket for a toilet, he was forced to do hard labor in a quarry. He was allowed one visitor a year for 30 minutes. He could write and receive one letter every six months. But Robben Island became the crucible which transformed him.

Through his intelligence, charm and dignified defiance, Mandela eventually bent even the most brutal prison officials to his will, assumed leadership over his jailed comrades and became the master of his own prison. He emerged from it the mature leader who would fight and win the great political battles that would create a new democratic South Africa.

"Especially for those of us who lived in single cells, you had the time to sit down and think, and we discovered that sitting down just to think is one of the best ways of keeping yourself fresh and able, to be able to address the problems facing you, and you had the opportunity, also, of examining your past."

-Nelson Mandela

He has received prestigious international awards, the freedom of many cities and honorary degrees from several universities. Musicians have been inspired to compose songs and music in his honor. Major international art exhibits have been dedicated to him and some of the most prominent writers have contributed to books for him and about him. Even an atomic particle has been named after him.

Mandela is a universal symbol of freedom and reconciliation, an icon representing the triumph of the human spirit. During his lifetime he not only dedicated himself to the struggle of the African people, but with his humility, and his spirit of forgiveness, he captured hearts and inspired people all over the world.

Nelson Mandela never wavered in his devotion to democracy, equality, and learning. Despite terrible provocation, he never answered racism with racism. His life is an inspiration to all who are oppressed and deprived, and to all who are opposed to oppression and deprivation.

Malala: The Girl Who Stood Up for Education and Was Shot by the Taliban

"I don't want to be thought of as the «girl who was shot by the Taliban» but the «girl who fought for education.» This is the cause to which I want to devote my life."
                                                        –Malala Yousafzai

As a young girl, Malala Yousafzai defied the Taliban in Pakistan and demanded that girls be allowed to receive an education. She was shot in the head by a Taliban gunman in 2012, but survived and went on to receive the Nobel Peace Prize.

Malala was born on 12 July 1997 in Mingora, a town in the Swat District of north-west Pakistan. Her father, Ziauddin Yousafzai named her after Malalai, a Pashtun heroine.

Ziauddin, who has always loved learning, ran a school in Swat adjacent to the family's home. He was known as an advocate for education in Pakistan, which has the second highest number of out of school children in the world and became an outspoken opponent of Taliban efforts to restrict education and stop girls from going to school.

"I told myself, Malala, you have already faced death. This is your second life. Don't be afraid — if you are afraid, you can't move forward."
                                                        –Malala Yousafzai

Malala and her father received death threats but continued to speak out for the right to education.

Malala became a global advocate for the millions of girls being denied a formal education because of social, economic, legal and political factors. In 2013, Malala and Ziauddin co-founded the Malala Fund to bring awareness to the social and economic impact of girls' education and to empower girls to raise their voices, to unlock their potential and to demand change.

Notably, the Malala Fund provides funding to the Centre for Girls' Education (CGE) in northern Nigeria to support hundreds of in- and out-of-school girls through learning clubs held in spaces supplied by the local community. In these "safe spaces" led by a local mentor, groups of girls are taught reading, writing, math, and life and livelihood skills.

"With guns, you can kill terrorists; with education, you can kill terrorism."
–Malala Yousafzai

Funding also supports CGE's provision of scholarships to cover school-related expenses for girls in secondary school. The program is reducing social and economic barriers to girls' education, helping to delay marriage, and expanding the critical years in which girls can acquire social assets and skills that will serve them as adults.

Malala accepted the Nobel Peace Prize on 10 December 2014 with Indian children's rights and education advocate Kailash Satyarthi. Malala contributed her entire prize money of more than $500,000 to financing the creation of a secondary school for girls in Pakistan.

"If people were silent nothing would change."

–Malala Yousafzai

If you are silent about the Problems around you, nothing will change

You must have noticed a trend throughout this chapter. They all stood for a problem. They all risked their lives in the process. They were the *'Josephs'*, the *'Caleb and Joshuas'* to their generations.

Dear reader, the world is in need of men and women like this, who are not afraid of problems. The world is in desperate need of men and women who have the right attitude towards problems. The world is in desperate need of problem solvers. Your nation desperately needs you to solve the problems in the land. And who knows, maybe you are here for such a time as this? Just like Mordecai challenged Esther.

The common feature of everyone you've just read about and a whole lot of others which space will not permit me to write about is that they all ended up in greatness. The problems they solved were the key to their prominence.

None! Not a single one of them lived a life of mediocrity afterwards.

Problem is a fast track to prominence, greatness and a life of significance. Your life will only be worth celebrating if you dedicate it to solving problems.

The world revolves around problems and only those who take these problems head on will be singled out for greatness. If you will remain silent about the problems around you, nothing will change.

In the next chapter, I will be showing you another key lesson you can derive from these stories because truly, problems and money are closely related but that's not the only thing that solving problems can do for you. There is a lot more. So, stay tuned!

Nuggets

1. Every one of us will not have any relevance or significance without solving one problem or the other.

2. I tell you this that not a single one of us will be needed if we live in a world without problems.

3. Be equipped to solve a problem. Stop complaining about problems. Instead, do extensive research on how to solve problems.

4. The world is in desperate need of men and women who have the right attitude towards problems. The world is in desperate need of problem solvers.

5. Your nation desperately needs you to solve the problems in the land. And who knows, maybe you are here for such a time as this?

6. The world revolves around problems and only those who take these problems head on will be singled out for greatness. If you will remain silent about the problems around you, nothing will change.

7. Problems and money are closely related but that's not the only thing that solving problems can do for you. There is a lot more.

CHAPTER 12

Getting rich is Automatic if you will solve Problems

Getting rich is Automatic if you will solve Problems

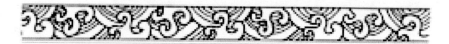

Nelson Mandela became very relevant and was even tagged a 'world citizen' because he fought apartheid. Malala fought for her right to education for herself and the Pakistani children. Martin Luther King Jr. stood against injustice and racial discrimination. Esther aborted the plot to kill her people even though her life was at risk. The Wright brothers gave the world one of the fastest means of transportation today.

Think of every one of them and all others you've read about in the course of this book and you will discover that their relevance was tied to the problems they solved. You will notice that without those problems they dedicated their lives to solving, the last chapter would have probably been filled with other names.

Take time to brood over this, what brought Bill Gates to the limelight? The problem of personal computers brought Bill Gates to prominence. And when there was another problem that computers are too big to carry about and we needed smaller, handier and better designs, Steve Jobs became relevant. Getting rich became automatic for both of them because of the problems they solved.

The people you read about in the last chapter might not be the richest. Some of them might not have made it to the Forbes list, but it is also important to note that the problems they solved were the keys to their wealth, relevance, significance, honor and prominence. And I will elaborate on the other things that could be associated with solving problems in this chapter.

Take this along with you

Meanwhile, I strongly believe that this book has been able to prove to you beyond reasonable doubt that money is always connected to problems. Money is a by-product of problems. And you must have also come to realize that there is a cordial relationship between problems and money.

I also believe that you already know by now that money and problems are very close relatives. The child of problem is solution and the grandchild of problem is money. Problems must give birth to solutions, then, the solution leads to money. Problem, therefore, is a wealthy goldmine. And where there is a problem, there is money.

Problem → Solution → Money

This has been the main theme of this book up until now. The story of Bata Shoe Company, the attitude of Caleb and Joshua, how the Chinese and Japanese firms have been taking advantage of the problems in Africa, the story of Henry Ford, the biblical story of Joseph and Esther have all proven that where there is a problem, there is money. They have also shown you how to see the opportunities hidden in problems.

More importantly, their stories are good examples on how to approach and come up with solutions to the problems you find around you. These are the stories that you read and you never worry about money again. They are the stories that will make you take responsibility for the problems around you. They are the stories that make you an employer of labor instead of looking for jobs.

That been said, there are still a lot more that could come along with solving problems and that is one of the main reasons why I shared the stories in the last chapter with you.

In addition to what I've been discussing with you so far that:

Wherever there is a problem, there is money

Wherever there is a problem, there is a job, and

Wherever there is a problem, there are opportunities;

I'll also like you to take this along with you.

Wherever there is a problem, there is honor

Whenever you see a problem that is your place of honor. The people we refer to as great or heroes are the problem solvers. They saw a problem and they responded. David became a hero because he saw Goliath and jumped on him. When two women were fighting over one child, King Solomon solved the problem and he was regarded as the wisest man on earth. Esther fearlessly and courageously fought for the Jews. What of the likes of Nelson Mandela, Malala, and Martin Luther King Jr.? They all became Nobel Laureates because of the problem they dedicated their lives to solving.

In the same light, over the past few years, the honors and accolades for Flying Doctors started by Dr. Ola have begun to flow, with the prestigious World Economic Forum recognizing her considerable achievements by naming her amongst its prestigious Young Global Leaders class of 2013, a group it describes as the best of today's leaders under the age of 40.

Jack Ma of Alibaba has been named one of the world's most influential people by Time Magazine in 2009, businessperson of the year in 2007 by Business week, Asia's Heroes of Philanthropy in 2010 by Forbes Asia, one of 30 world's best CEOs by Barron's in 2008 and in 2001, he made the list of young global leaders by the World Economic Forum.

What of Sam Walton of Walmart? Just before Walton's passing, he received the Medal of Freedom, from President George H. W. Bush. This is an honor reserved for the nation's most respected civilians.

Wherever there is a problem, there is honor hidden there. As soon as the problem is resolved, you become the hero. Behind every problem, there is honor hidden there. Whenever you resolve any problem, honor comes to you. Whenever you resolve any problem, respect comes to you. Whenever you resolve any problem, you become relevant. Whenever you provide an answer to a problem, you become significant in the society.

The reason why people will respect you is because of the problem you solve. Those who complain, groan and do nothing about the problem in the society are often met with disrespect and dishonor.

Wherever you see a problem, there is a blessing

Wherever you see a problem, there is a blessing. Blessings always come in unexpected manners. Blessings are always disguised. If you see the raw diamond, it is like dirt. More so, you need to dig deep into the soil to get it.

Deep down in the depth of every dirt, there is a diamond. Hidden under every problem is a blessing. Whenever there is a problem, there is a blessing and a provision.

There was a problem in Egypt. Pharaoh wanted an interpretation to his dream. Nobody could give an answer to the problem but Joseph did. That problem became a blessing for Joseph. He went from slavery in the prison to become the Prime Minister, and Egypt became the economic hub of the world during the famine, thanks to problems!

Wherever there is a problem, there is a future

Wherever there is a problem, there is a future. This is true because if you are down already, you can only go up. If there are problems, it means things are down. If the economy has problems, it means the economy is down. The only place anything that is 'down' can go is 'up.' And if it's up already, the only place it can go is down.

Are you still running away from the third world countries? Are you still running away from places that are associated with so many problems? Are you still running away from Africa? Are you still running away from Nigeria? Are you still blaming the government? Are you still complaining? Are you still waiting for the future or you will stand up and create it?

Well, I am running to Africa. Africa is the future, my dear. It is the wealthiest goldmine in the world right now. The future is where there are a lot of problems. The future is in Africa. We are going to create that future. We are not going to wait till there is electricity, water, and everything are provided. No! Everything there right now is only temporal.

Even the Bible confirms this in 2 Corinthians 4:18:

"While we look not at the things which are seen, but at the things which are not seen: for the things which are seen are temporal; but the things which are not seen are eternal."

If it is poverty that is there right now, it is temporal. It shall be replaced with wealth. If it is hunger that is widespread right now, it is temporal. It shall be replaced with abundance. Wherever there is a problem, there is a future.

Just a quick recap:

Wherever there is a problem, there is money

Wherever there is a problem, there is a job

Wherever there is a problem, there are opportunities

Wherever there is a problem, there is honor

Wherever you see a problem, there is a blessing, and

Wherever there is a problem, there is a future.

The future is in Africa

The future is in Africa, my dear. Or do you think a man like Aliko Dangote, the richest African was disillusioned when he said something like this;

"If you give me $5 billion today, I will not invest any abroad, I will invest everything here in Nigeria."

Also in one of his interviews on CNN, he was quoted as saying,

"Nigeria is the best place to invest. It is one of the best places in the world where you can make money."

This is coming from a man that represents what African businessmen should be. He is an example for aspiring entrepreneurs across the continent. He is a problem solver.

Take a quick look at the number of problems he is solving presently in the Nigerian economy. The Dangote consortium spans across numerous sectors of the Nigerian economy. The Dangote Group supplies commodities like cement, sugar, salt, flour, rice, spaghetti, fabric etc. at very competitive prices. He practically took the responsibility upon himself to supply basic needs to a country of about 180million individuals.

If you don't use Dangote sugar, you probably use Dangote salt or flour to cook. And if you are not putting on a cloth that came from Dangote fabric, you are most likely living in a house built with Dangote cement.

In fact, it may possibly not be a wild assumption to say that all Nigerians have heard of his name due to the impact of his business. His goods are practically in most homes across the country. People who may not use his products might have passed a few of his trailers by the way.

The sugar refinery at Apapa port, Lagos is the largest in Africa and in size the third largest worldwide with an annual capacity of 700,000 tonnes of refined sugar annually.

Dangote textile and the Nigeria Textiles Mills Plc, which it acquired, produce over 120,000 meters of finished textiles daily. The group has a ginnery in Kankawa, Katsina State with a capacity of 30,000 MT of seeded cotton annually. The Dangote group also boasts about the Obajana Cement plant which is the largest cement manufacturing facility in Africa.

Instead of stashing his funds in foreign accounts, a typical feature of fraudulent front and public office looters, Dangote invests wisely in the productive sector of the Nigerian economy. To deny that Dangote doesn't have a monopoly over a few of the commodities in the Nigerian market is to deny the obvious.

What of Mike Adenuga? Michael Adeniyi Adenuga Jr. popularly called Mike Adenuga is a Nigerian business tycoon and the second richest person in Nigeria.

His telecommunication company, Globacom is Nigeria's second-largest telecom operator, and also has a presence in Ghana and Benin. He also owns stakes in The Equitorial Trust Bank and the oil exploration firm, Conoil (formerly Consolidated Oil Company).

Forbes has estimated his net worth at $3.2 billion as of September 2015 which makes him the second wealthiest Nigerian behind Aliko Dangote, and the sixth richest person in Africa, thanks to the businesses he has set up to solve pressing problems in the country.

And when you go to the entertainment and information industry, the name of Linda Ikeji pops up. Linda Ikeji has earned herself the title 'Queen of Blogging.' Lindaikeji's blog has grown to be one of the most visited sites in the country. As a regular source for news, entertainment, celebrity gist, gossip and much more, her blog continues to attract thousands of visitors.

In August 2012, Forbes Africa described her as a success and a case study for the business of blogging. Her blog gets over 50,000 visits daily and is a hot spot for online advertisers and people wishing to attract web traffic to their websites or blogs. This makes her the highest earning blogger in Nigeria.

Also in the African entertainment industry is a man that has created a niche for himself. Born 1982, Jason Njoku is an internet entrepreneur and has a net worth of approximately $30 million US. He is presently one of the most successful internet entrepreneurs in Africa. He is the CEO and founder of Iroko partners, the largest distributor of Nigerian music and movies online.

So what problem gave birth to Iroko TV? Jason first noticed his mother had gone from watching western movies to watching African movies. But here comes the problem, he realized his mother and other relatives had difficulties getting their hands on their beloved movies from Nigeria's booming Nollywood industry. And this gave birth to Iroko online TV in October 2010. To date, Iroko partners still remain YouTube's largest partner in Africa.

The Iroko TV site has recorded over 800,000 registered users as of 2013, and over 14 million hours of movies have been watched in 178 countries around the world.

Iroko Partners was also one of the first companies in the Nigerian digital music scene, launching iROKING in 2011. The platform has almost 100,000 registered users who have access to over 35,000 tracks by 400+ artists. As of 2013, across all the Iroko Partners' platforms, 193,000,000 minutes of entertainment are consumed every month.

This problem he has taken upon himself to solve has made him one of Africa's Top Young Millionaires to watch by Forbes Africa. He has also been named as one of London's Top Black Men of Power in Black Enterprise Magazine.

And his advice to the young African entrepreneurs in the making:

"Don't wait around – the sector is in its infancy but that doesn't mean it's not going to move quickly. There are a lot of people out there who are smarter than me, who have an Ivy-League education and who have great ideas to start up a business, but something is holding them back and they are voyeurs rather than entrepreneurs. My advice to young entrepreneurs is this: don't wait for the day when you're reading about YOUR idea in the business pages. Do it now. Break free from the shackles that hold you back and start your business today"

My dear friend, the future is in Africa. Most of our industries and various sectors of our economy are still in its infancy. Don't wait until someone else is solving the problem you are meant to solve. Don't wait until someone else is making millions out of your ideas. There are still a lot of problems in Africa crying for solutions and you know that those solutions will bring you unfathomable wealth because the demand is much and the problems are a lot. Where there is a problem, there will always be money.

You don't have to attend an Ivy-League school. You don't have to be the smartest among your peers. All that is required of you is to come up with efficient solutions to the pressing problems around you. Remember, Jason Njoku did not have to look too far away for a problem to solve. He just observed his mum and his relatives and that changed his financial status.

Worrying is a waste of Time

In the early 1990s, Donald Trump was near $1 billion in debt personally and $9 billion in debt corporately. An interviewer asked him if he was worried. He replied, *"Worrying is a waste of time. Worrying gets in my way of working to solve problems."*

As I conclude, I will like to leave you with this. Instead of worrying, look around for what needs to be done, seek out the problems that are crying for solutions around you and solve them. Then and only then will you experience God's abundance beyond your imagination.

Stop running away from problems. Actually, whatever you are looking for in life is hidden in the problems you resolve. Are you looking for honor? You will find it in problems. Are you looking for opportunities? You will find it in problems. Are you looking for jobs? You will find them in problems. Are you looking for a future and destiny? You will find them in problems. Are you looking for blessings? You will find them in problems. Chase after problems. Embrace it. Welcome it and find solutions to it.

If you train yourself to begin to look for problems and look for ways to resolve them, you will experience God's blessings and have much more honor than you could ever imagine. And you will discover that getting rich is automatic if you will solve problems.

Wherever there is a problem, there is money!

Blessings!

Nuggets

1. Behind every problem, there is honor hidden there.

2. Whenever you provide an answer to a problem, you become significant in the society.

3. The reason why people will respect you is because of the problem you solve. Those who complain, groan and do nothing about the problem in the society are often met with disrespect and dishonor.

4. Hidden under every problem is a blessing. Whenever there is a problem, there is a blessing and a provision.

5. Are you still waiting for the future or you will stand up and create it?

6. Whatever you are looking for in life is hidden in the problems you resolve.

7. If you train yourself to begin to look for problems and look for ways to resolve them, you will experience God's blessings and have much more honor than you could ever imagine. And you will discover that getting rich is automatic if you will solve problems.

Final Thoughts

There is a popular adage that says, *"You can teach a child to memorize the word 'bicycle' but you cannot teach a child to ride one. A child needs to learn how to ride a bicycle by doing."*

This book has been written as a guide on how to recognize opportunities and the possibilities associated with solving problems. But the actual process of recognizing a problem around you and solving such problems is a process you have to undertake yourself.

The more you try to do this on your own, every single day and at every time, the more your ability to solve problems will increase. Over time you will begin to see solutions to problems that the average person never sees. And before you know it you will begin to experience the abundance of money associated with being a problem solver.

When we learn to ride a bicycle, we train our subconscious mind to ride our bike. Once that is done, we don't have to think or remember how to ride a bike as we ride. When we learn to drive a car, we also train our subconscious mind. That is why, once we have trained our subconscious mind to drive, we can drive and talk to someone else, eat a hamburger, think about other things or listen to the radio and sing along. Driving is automatically handled. The same can happen with recognizing a problem and coming up with the best solution to that problem.

What takes the longest time to do is getting your mind to think solutions instead of worrying or complaining about problems. But the good news is that since you've digested the contents of this book, your attitude and the way you now see problems will make solving problems easier. Not only does it get easier, but the solutions you will begin to come up with will be mind blowing. And this is because you've trained your mind to always automatically think solutions whenever you sense or see a problem around.

Getting rich is automatic if you will solve problems. I therefore, welcome you to a new reality where you can experience God's abundance by solving the pressing and really painful problems around you.

Welcome to a world where you never have to worry about money again!

Thank you for reading this far. I really can't wait to hear what becomes of you through the application of the wisdom nuggets contained in this book. Feel free to write me anytime, I read every single mail and will be glad to reply you.

pastor @godembassy.org

You can also avail yourself of other training materials of mine on my blog:

www.SundayAdelajaBlog.com

FOR THE LOVE OF GOD, CHURCH, AND NATION

SUNDAY ADELAJA'S
BIOGRAPHY

Pastor Sunday Adelaja is the Founder and Senior Pastor of The Embassy of the Blessed Kingdom of God for All Nations Church in Kyiv, Ukraine.

Sunday Adelaja is a Nigerian-born Leader, Thinker, Philosopher, Transformation Strategist, Pastor, Author and Innovator who lives in Kiev, Ukraine.

At 19, he won a scholarship to study in the former Soviet Union. He completed his master's program in Belorussia State University with distinction in journalism.

At 33, he had built the largest evangelical church in Europe — The Embassy of the Blessed Kingdom of God for All Nations.

Sunday Adelaja is one of the few individuals in our world who has been privileged to speak in the United Nations, Israeli Parliament, Japanese Parliament and the United States Senate.

The movement he pioneered has been instrumental in reshaping lives of people in the Ukraine, Russia and about 50 other nations where he has his branches.

His congregation, which consists of ninety-nine percent white Europeans, is a cross-cultural model of the church for the 21st century.

His life mission is to advance the Kingdom of God on earth by raising a generation of history makers who will live for a cause larger, bigger and greater than themselves. Those who will live like Jesus and transform every sphere of the society in every nation as a model of the Kingdom of God on earth.

His economic empowerment program has succeeded in raising over 200 millionaires in the short period of three years.

Sunday Adelaja is the author of over 300 books, many of which are translated into several languages including Russian, English, French, Chinese, German, etc.

His work has been widely reported by world media outlets such as The Washington Post, The Wall Street Journal, New York Times, Forbes, Associated Press, Reuters, CNN, BBC, German, Dutch and French national television stations.

Pastor Sunday is happily married to his "Princess" Bose Dere-Adelaja. They are blessed with three children: Perez, Zoe and Pearl.

Bill Clinton —
42Nd President Of The
United States (1993–2001),
Former Arcansas State
Governor

Ariel "Arik" Sharon —
Israeli Politician, Israeli
Prime Minister (2001–2006)

Benjamin Netanyahu —
Statesman Of Israel. Israeli
Prime Minister (1996–1999),
Acting Prime Minister
(From 2009)

Jean ChrEtien —
Canadian Politician,
20Th Prime Minister Of
Canada, Minister Of Justice
Of Canada, Head Of Liberan
Party Of Canada

Rudolph Giuliani —
American Political Actor,
Mayor Of New York Served
From 1994 To 2001. Actor
Of Republican Party

Colin Powell —
Is An American Statesman
And A Retired Four-Star
General In The Us Army,
65Th United States Secretary
Of State

Peter J. Daniels —
Is A Well-Known And
Respected Australian
Christian International
Business Statesman Of
Substance

Madeleine
Korbel Albright —
An American Politician And
Diplomat, 64[Th] United States
Secretary Of State

Kenneth Robert
Livingstone —
An English Politician,
1[St] Mayor Of London
(4 May 2000 – 4 May
2008), Labour Party
Representative

Sir Richard Charles Nicholas Branson — English Business Magnate, Investor And Philanthropist. He Founded The *Virgin Group*, Which Controls More Than 400 Companies

Mel Gibson — American Actor And Filmmaker

Chuck Norris — American Martial Artist, Actor, Film Producer And Screenwriter

Christopher Tucker —
American Actor
And Comedian

Bernice Albertine King —
American Minister Best
Known As The Youngest
Child Of Civil Rights Leaders
Martin Luther King Jr. And
Coretta Scott King Andrew

Andrew Young — American
Politician, Diplomat, And
Activist, 14Th United States
Ambassador To The United
Nations, 55Th Mayor Of
Atlanta

General Wesley
Kanne Clark —
4-Star General And Nato
Supreme Allied Commander

Dr. Sunday Adelaja's family:
Perez, Pearl, Zoe and Pastor Bose Adelaja

FOLLOW
SUNDAY ADELAJA
ON SOCIAL MEDIA

Subscribe And Read Pastor Sunday's Blog:
www.sundayadelajablog.com

**Follow these links and listen to over 200
of Pastor Sunday's Messages free of charge:**
http://sundayadelajablog.com/content/

Follow Pastor Sunday on Twitter:
www.twitter.com/official_pastor

Join Pastor Sunday's Facebook
page to stay in touch:
www.facebook.com/
pastor.sunday.adelaja

Visit our websites for more
information about Pastor
Sunday's ministry:
http://www.godembassy.com
http://www.
pastorsunday.com
http://sundayadelaja.de

CONTACT

BEST SELLING BOOKS BY DR. SUNDAY ADELAJA
AVAILABLE ON AMAZON.COM AND OKADABOOKS.COM

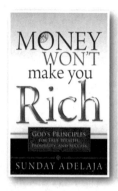

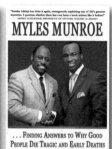
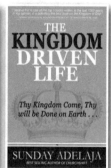

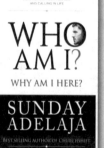

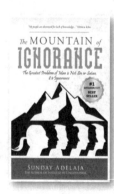

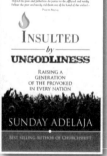
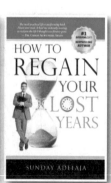

Best Selling Books by Dr. Sunday Adelaja
Available on Amazon.com and Okadabooks.com

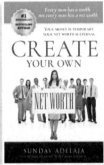
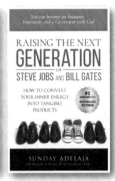
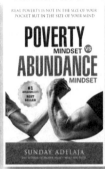

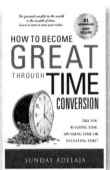
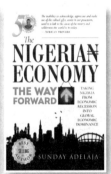
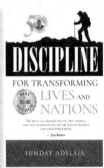

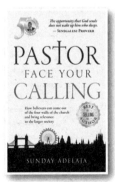

FOR DISTRIBUTION OR TO ORDER BULK COPIES OF THIS BOOKS, PLEASE CONTACT US:

USA | CORNERSTONE PUBLISHING
E-mail: info@thecornerstonepublishers.com, +1 (516) 547-4999
www.thecornerstonepublishers.com

AFRICA | SUNDAY ADELAJA MEDIA LTD.
E-mail: btawolana@hotmail.com
+2348187518530, +2348097721451, +2348034093699

LONDON, UK | PASTOR ABRAHAM GREAT
E-mail: abrahamagreat@gmail.com, +447711399828, +441908538141

KIEV, UKRAINE |
E-mail: pa@godembassy.org, Mobile: +380674401958

GOLDEN JUBILEE SERIES BOOKS
BY DR. SUNDAY ADELAJA

FOR DISTRIBUTION OR TO ORDER BULK COPIES OF THIS BOOKS, PLEASE CONTACT US:

USA | CORNERSTONE PUBLISHING
E-mail: info@thecornerstonepublishers.com, +1 (516) 547-4999
www.thecornerstonepublishers.com

AFRICA | SUNDAY ADELAJA MEDIA LTD.
E-mail: btawolana@hotmail.com
+2348187518530, +2348097721451, +2348034093699

LONDON, UK | PASTOR ABRAHAM GREAT
E-mail: abrahamagreat@gmail.com, +447711399828, +441908538141

KIEV, UKRAINE |
E-mail: pa@godembassy.org, Mobile: +380674401958